BILLY ROBINSON WITH JAKE SHANNON

PHYSICAL CHESS

MY LIFE IN CATCH-AS-CATCH-CAN WRESTLING

Published by ECW Press
2120 Queen Street East, Suite 200, Toronto, Ontario, Canada M4E 1E2
416-694-3348 / info@ecwpress.com

LIBRARY AND ARCHIVES CANADA CATALOGUING IN PUBLICATION

Robinson, Billy, 1938-
Physical chess : my life in catch-as-catch-can wrestling / Billy
Robinson and Jake Shannon.

ISBN 978-1-77041-062-6
ALSO ISSUED AS: 978-1-77090-214-5 (PDF); 978-1-77090-215-2 (EPUB)

1. Robinson, Billy, 1938- 2. Wrestlers—Great Britain—Biography.
3. Coaches (Athletics)—Biography. 4. Mixed martial arts—Biography.

1. Shannon, Jake II. Title.

GV1196.R635A3 2012   796.812092   C2011-906982-2

Editor for the press: Michael Holmes
Cover design: Cyanotype
Cover images: Fumi
Interior images: photographs on pages 8, 27, 43, 85, 107, 116, 117, 118, 119, 120, 122, 123, 126, 127, 130, 132, 133, and 138 courtesy of Fumi; all other images courtesy of Billy Robinson.
Text design and typesetting: Troy Cunningham
Printing: Thomson-Shore   1   2   3   4   5

PRINTED AND BOUND IN THE UNITED STATES

CONTENTS

FOREWORD

You hold in your hands a treasure. As someone who has
very sincerely devoted the last decade to researching
the sport of catch-as-catch-can (and to learning its
secrets first-hand from the tough old-timers who prac-
tised this sport), I realize how lucky we are to have
this piece of history from the most successful of the
last Lancashire catch-as-catch-can wrestlers, Billy
Robinson. Studying this art has been frustrating
because those seeking their fortunes in the scripted
world of twentieth-century professional wrestling
have manipulated the history so much.

"Kayfabe" and the mentality of "protecting the
business," while perhaps entertaining, have taken us
far from the facts. This book stands nearly alone as a

true testament to those wrestlers who risked life and limb practising the dangerous sport of catch-as-catch-can wrestling without ever achieving the fame or fortune associated with "worked" pro wrestling.

I am going to assume that you haven't heard of the majority of the people mentioned in this book. Here Billy does the memory of many a tough wrestler, as well as the history of wrestling, a tremendous service in familiarizing the modern reader with little-known greats from the past. These are the men who broke their bones, spilled their blood, and bet the wages they earned after a long day in the coal mines, steel mills, or lumber-yards, merely to see who was the better man.

Billy's story is absolutely fascinating—from his encounter with Hemingway in Spain and his travels the world over, wrestling all comers, to his life as a professional wrestler and his pivotal role in the birth of the modern Mixed Martial Arts movement. How many people can say they've travelled the world all expenses paid, starred in a Hollywood movie, been a pro wrestling and amateur wrestling champion, and trained some of the greatest MMA fighters the world has ever seen?

Having Billy as a friend and resource over the years has changed my view not just of wrestling, but also of the world, and it is my earnest hope that this book will bring you closer to the kind, smart, and tough man better known as "the British Lion," Billy Robinson.

JAKE SHANNON

CHAPTER ONE
BEGINNINGS

I come from a fighting family. My great-great-grandfather Harry Robinson was a bare-knuckle boxing champion of Great Britain, which in those days really meant world champion. My uncle Alf boxed with the world heavyweight champion Max Baer and wrestled another world heavyweight champion, Jack Sherry, in Belgium. And then there's my

Alf Robinson after turning pro in wrestling upon retiring from boxing.

father, a street fighter turned pro who fought the black American boxer Tiger Flowers and was once world light heavyweight champion. Tiger told my father that he was the strongest man Tiger had ever fought.

In those days, fighters were known around the country. *They* were the stars, not soccer players, not rugby players. It was fighters and wrestlers—Billy Riley, Joe and Bob Robinson, Charlie Carroll, the Carroll brothers, the Belshaw brothers, Pop Charnock, and too many others to name—that people revered. Those guys were legends, and they were unbelievable athletes. Unfortunately, nobody really kept fight records that long ago, so the names of so many great wrestlers have been lost forever.

The number of forgotten wrestlers, let alone champions, is staggering.

THE TIMES WERE TOUGH BACK THEN!

I was born in 1938. We had just gone through two wars—the Boer War and the First World War—and the third was about to begin. Life was rough. My siblings, both elder to me, would die in bombings during the Second World War. I never got to know them. My granddad—that is, my dad's dad—had died in the trenches during the 1914–1918 war. My dad had to take care of his family when he was about 11 or 12. He got into the green grocery business (green grocery means fruit and vegetables, certain canned stuff and fish and fowl). I remember that I hated Christmas as a kid because my job in those days was plucking and cleaning turkeys, geese, and chickens. That's what I did all through Christmas. I didn't want to look at a table and see a turkey or a chicken that I'd plucked. At one time, my dad had a number of shops. He put all his brothers and sisters into the business, and he would buy for all the shops.

It's difficult to explain today how tough it was then just to survive. The industrial age had started, but the unions had not yet got enough power to make life and conditions easier for the working class people. On the average day, a major meal was beans on toast with a fried egg on top, or fish and chips, or a sandwich with a mug of tea. Maybe, on a Sunday, you'd be able to

Billy Riley with the Championship Belt.

afford a roast, and that was considered a family feast. The average life expectancy for a male in Wigan in the 1920s and '30s was about 23 or 24 years, and for a female it was not much more than 30 (I read this in an old Wigan newspaper when I was training there with Billy Riley). People had huge families, but a lot of children died from diphtheria and other diseases whose cures we now take for granted, and this kept the average size of a family down. There were also a lot of coal mine accidents.

People would do anything to make money. Back then, betting on anything was legitimate. They'd bet on "barrel jumping" (standing jumps into lined-up empty beer kegs), "ratting" contests (killing rats with their teeth), or "purring" matches (kicking each other wearing coal mining boots or wooden shoes with metal rims until one gave in or broke a leg).

Wigan, 1930s

"Hop, step, and a jump" was a big deal at the time. There's this funny story about an old-timer who had retired as the champion of hop, step, and a jump. The new champion came up and was ridiculing him and his accomplishments. Finally, the old-timer said, "Okay, I'll tell you what I'll do. We will make the bet that you cannot out-jump me, if I can pick where we jump." The young kid and his backers said, "Yeah." So the bet was made. The old-timer took them to the top of a seven-storey factory, and he jumped a hop, step and a jump, and his toes were hanging over the edge of the building. The only way the kid was going to win was if he jumped over the edge and killed himself. That's a true story. That's how people were back then.

Wrestlers had private matches on bowling greens on weekends. Most pubs had a bowling green because in England we play bowls on the grass, and on Sundays everything was closed. Side bets on these matches supplemented wrestlers' incomes; they had private matches for a week's wage or whatever they could afford. That meant one guy's family was going to eat next to nothing the following week. Only the wrestlers' friends and people making private side-stake bets were allowed to watch the match.

Then there were street fights, which were private matches in locker rooms. Men would go in and lock the door. People bet on who'd come out. My dad was the number one street fighter during his day. I learned so much from him.

There were no distractions for kids, because there were no cell phones, no television, and no video games. There was very little radio. I remember when

I was seven or eight years old, we'd play knock-a-door and run away and hide, watching people come out to see who it was. Once, I tipped over bottles of milk. This was probably 1945, just at the end of the war. Milk was hard to get, and we used to have milk people that would come with the bottles and leave them outside the front doors. The people of the house heard the crash and saw me and my friends running away. They knew who I was and called on my dad.

He was waiting for me and my friends when I came home. He asked me, "What you been doing?"

The lady from the house said, "Well, they kicked my milk over."

So he asked me, "Billy, did you do that?" But I didn't answer.

Now, my friend Billy Hubble didn't want me to get into trouble, so he said, "Mr. Robinson, I did it."

But the lady said, "No, he didn't. Your son did it."

So I said, "Okay."

My dad paid for the damage I had caused, and he totally ignored me for

What a competitive wrestler used to look like.

a week. When I spoke to him, he looked through me like I wasn't even there. Boy, I felt so bad about that. It was a lot worse than any physical punishment—my dad never hit me in his life. In our family, nobody lied or got out of anything that they had done. They all owned up to what they had done.

Back then, you had to make your own entertainment. On Sundays when the family decided to get together, everybody came over to our house, at the shop in Manchester. We always had a piano, a concertina, a banjo, and an accordion. My dad played all kinds of different instruments. Everyone in the family played something. I played piano and alto saxophone.

Everyone would gather around and play. Afterwards, my mother cooked for everybody. She was a hairdresser and a good cook. Somebody would bring desserts. The kids played together, the men had a few drinks and smoke, and the women spent time together. Later on, everyone gathered around the piano with all the different instruments and sang. And that would be it. They'd all go home and the kids would go to bed.

Well into the 1930s, about 30 percent of the Western world was illiterate. Educated people didn't make that much money. In my dad's era, it was always said that a person with common sense was going to be far better off than an educated person with no common sense. My mother wanted me to be educated, but my father was more into teaching me to look after myself and advance in a world of, shall we say, semi-educated people. I did two years of college at a private school, so I got the idea of what it was like, but my father decided that he wasn't going to pay for any more, because he thought it was a waste of time.

Obviously, times have changed dramatically. Take, for example, my son, Spencer. He's the pride of my life. I put Spencer through private school. There was no wrestling in private school, but he did get a fellowship to West Point, and now he's a lieutenant colonel in the National Guard, and he's doing very, very well for

Billy's son Spencer trying the World's Heavyweight Championship on for size.

himself. He grew up to be a lot taller than I am, and he had to become an American to go to West Point, so now not only does he look down at me, he also calls me a "bloody foreigner."

HOW I BECAME A CATCH-AS-CATCH-CAN WRESTLER

My father never wanted me to get into boxing or wrestling. Or, at least, I'll put it this way: he may have wanted it, but he never let me know it, just as I never pushed Spencer to do it. But circumstances made sure I got into wrestling.

By the end of the war, a lot of guys were involved in the black market, making money selling anything from silk stockings to gas coupons, watches, and so on. And when you walked through the streets, there was always a chance that you might be seeing something that they didn't want you to see, and they'd attack you and beat you up. So the first thing I learned in street fighting was to get a 4H pencil (its lead is very hard, so it doesn't lose its point), sharpen it, stick it about four inches out of my hand, and then roll my shoulder (my dad taught me how) and flick it straight out with the pencil aimed right for the eyes or the throat or cheek. So no matter what kind of roundhouse punches the attacker was sending my way, I could go *bump* and hit him in the eye or through the cheek or on his throat. That would stop anybody, and you could not get arrested for it because the pencil wasn't a weapon. If it were a knife, you could be arrested. Even back then, handguns and knives were illegal. There were no handguns, and very few people had knives. If you got caught with a knife over a certain length, that was an automatic jail sentence. My dad taught me a few other little things, like how to pivot, doing a 180-degree turn on the ball of your foot.

One day when I was really young, three kids chased me home. I was scared and crying. When I got home, my dad was there, asking, "Why are you crying?"

I said, "These kids are going to beat me up."

He said, "Have they touched you yet?"

I said, "No."

He said, "Well, fight them."

I said, "Dad, there's three of them."

He said, "Listen. You've got two choices. You can fight them, or you can fight me." And I didn't want to even think about that. He said, "Don't worry about it. You'll fight one at a time. I'll make sure it's one at a time." So he made me fight them one at a time and told me to remember what he had shown me.

It worked. And that's when I realized that all this stuff he'd been showing me was really effective. I beat the first kid down. The second kid, I hit him once, and he didn't want any more. The third one didn't fight. That was the first time I knew my dad was proud of something I'd done. So I felt pretty good about that. Then my dad took us all out for ice cream and loaded

Alf and Billy's father holding the Lonsdale belt at the Smithfield Market in Manchester, England [LEFT]; Billy's father (right) and Alf admiring the Lonsdale belt [RIGHT].

Lord Lonsdale Championship Trophy and two smiling guys.

them up with fruit from the shop to take home, because two of them had black eyes.

There were certain rules that you abided by in

Billy Robinson with IWA World Heavyweight Championship belt, Jack Robinson holding the Lonsdale Trophy, and Alf Robinson with the British Champion Lonsdale belt.

England in those days. Guys would go to the pub, and if someone had a dispute they would say, "Come on, let's go out to the cobbles." This basically meant, "Let's go out to the cobbled street, beat the hell out of each other, and then come back in and buy each other a drink." There was no animosity afterwards. To start a fight in a pub in England was very simple. You went to any pub in England, you drank your beer and then just turned the glass upside down. That meant you

Alf Robinson coaching his son Jack and his nephew Billy.

could beat anybody in the house; it was a challenge. Everybody understood these rules.

I always wanted to be a boxer. My uncle was a boxer, my dad was a boxer, and my great-grandfather was a bare-knuckle fighter. My dad used to take me to a pro boxing gym. I loved sparring. I started going through the training stuff at that time. I was going to be a boxer. Or so I thought.

One day, when I was 12 or 13, I was working at my dad's shop after school, straightening out crates and potato sacks to take back to the market the following morning. Other kids were playing with some Coca-Cola signs and spinning them through the air. Somebody shouted, "Look out, Billy!" I turned around, and one of the spinning things hit me in the eye. I don't remember much after that. It tore the retina from two o'clock all the way around to ten o'clock, and I was in the hospital for six months. That, of course, ended my boxing dream; there was no way I could get a boxing licence with the eye injury.

Fortunately, I used to watch my uncle when he wrestled in Manchester, and I used to go to the YMCA with my dad as a guest. This was a very exciting time for me as a kid because I was always around great professional fighters. I got to go to the gym with one of the all-time great catch-as-catch-can wrestlers from America, Benny Sherman. He would go with my dad to the gym because he was very interested in the street fighting aspect. He also sparred with different pro boxers. Sherman was great. Famous ballet-dancer-turned-wrestler Ricky Starr was also there, boxing with sparring partners like Rocky Graziano. Starr was a state amateur wrestling champion. He was a very good boxer, too. As a kid, I remember sitting on George Gregory's back while he was swimming laps. I personally knew people like Randy Turpin and Henry Cooper very well. A couple of other boxers also went there. My dad and all those guys worked out together, and I watched. I learned what it was like—the street fighting, the boxing, and then the wrestling.

By 14 years old, I was getting big. I was about six-foot-one, probably 180 pounds (remember, this is in England, where we are not as big as Americans as a whole), and I was in pretty good shape. My uncle Alf wanted to get me into pro wrestling, but my dad was in favor of trying me out at amateur wrestling first.

It wasn't until the 1960s that promoters put money into amateur wrestling. Until the mid-'60s, there was no amateur fighter—boxer or wrestler—who could compare with the pros, because there was no money in it. Whenever somebody got any good at a sport, they turned pro to make extra money for their family.

My dad took me down to the YMCA and introduced me to the coach of the amateur team. I stayed there. I had always been athletic, and with what I already knew about street fighting, boxing, and wrestling, it didn't take me long before I could hold my own with anybody there. At 14 or 15, I was beating 30-year-olds, and I thought, "Well, I come from a fighting family. It's in my blood."

Again my uncle wanted me to turn professional, but my dad said, "Look. If you're going to learn to wrestle, learn the best style that there is, the best form of combat fighting, which is catch-as-catch-can wrestling. And the greatest gym in the world is in Wigan, run by a man called Billy Riley."

At Billy Riley's gym (Karl Gotch called it "the Snake Pit," and the name stuck), I started out working with the wrestler Jack Dempsey (not the boxer), a.k.a. Tommy Moore, and with John Foley. John was a middleweight. Dempsey was a welterweight. These guys were older. They looked in shape, but they were too small. Or so I thought. I thought, "Well, he's only a welterweight, he's only a middleweight, I can handle these guys," because anybody that size in the YMCA, I had beaten very easily. What a mistake that was!

Billy asked me, "Well, what's your best hold?" At that time it was called a crucifix—it's where the opponent's in a defensive position on his hands and knees and you hook his arm by putting your leg around it and get a farther half nelson to turn him onto his back. I was a very strong young man; I had long, lanky arms and I was supple, so that was usually a very easy hold for me to get. But every time I tried it on these guys, I was on my back or screaming. The worst part was how easily they beat me. And of course Billy Riley and my dad were laughing. Finally Billy said, "Okay. You can start. We'll teach you." So it is that I learned to play physical chess.

Billy Riley, coach.

CHAPTER TWO
WIGAN DAYS

I started at Billy Riley's gym when I was 15 and was there for probably 12 years. When I began, Jack Dempsey, John Foley, and Joe Carroll were there. I was about 190 pounds, in great shape, and stood at six-foot-two. Billy Riley said, "Try it with this old guy." Well, the old guy—Charlie Carroll—was in his early fifties, about 155 or 160 pounds. I got on the mat with him. God! I've never got hurt so much in my life. He beat me very easily.

At times, I was able to take him down or get behind him and get control, or what I thought was control, for a short while. But every time I took him down, I got hurt. Every time he took me down, I got hurt. I'd land on an elbow or a knee (his). He'd have an ankle submission on me when I thought I was beating him. It was just unbelievable. Even after I had won the British Amateur Championship, when I went to the gym the next day Joe was there, and I went, "Oh, shit!" He kept me humble. It only got better when I started to understand what catch was all about and why he was beating me or why I was basically beating or hurting myself.

ABOUT CATCH-AS-CATCH-CAN

Lancashire-style wrestling, or catch-as-catch-can, was started by coal miners and steelworkers in the north of England. Guys who travelled the world, like those in the army and the navy, started to pick up all kinds of different fighting techniques, and that's how Wigan wrestlers found a style that beat all the different combat styles—more or less what MMA is becoming today, but with no time limits.

Four thousand years ago, the Greeks had a term for the Olympic Games; they called it "Agon." In the original Greek Olympics, whoever won the wrestling event was the champion of the Olympic Games. The Greeks had the best, most brutal submission wrestlers in that area of the world then. From drawings, we know that they used many of the same submissions we use today, and they were so good at it that the English word for pain, "agony," comes from this ancient Greek tradition.

I've heard people say Greco-Roman style, which

is a style of wrestling where you can't use your legs, came from Greece and Rome. In fact, the style was originally formed by the Vikings, the Nordic men. Denmark, Sweden, Finland, Norway, Lapland, and Estonia in those days were together called the Nordic countries. Some men fought with swords, but their most-used weapon was a double-headed battle axe, which was very heavy. They also had to do a lot of rowing, so they needed a lot of upper body strength. The Vikings formed a style of wrestling that developed the upper body. It became known as Greco-Roman in the modern Olympics in 1896, when they needed a name for it. Because the Olympics originated in Greece and Rome, they decided to call it Greco-Roman. There was no such thing as Greco-Roman wrestling before 1896.

Submission wrestling has been very important to the world. Wars have been decided by wrestling. Wars between tribes in Africa, between South American Indians, between peoples all over the world have been settled by the champion of one group fighting the champion of the other, sometimes to the death. It has saved thousands of lives that would have been lost otherwise. Henry VIII of England, for example, was a wrestling champion in his youth. He challenged the king of France to a wrestling match during a dispute over who should rule France. They wrestled, Henry lost, and the rest is history.

Henry VIII was from the Tudor family that brought

education to the people. The last order he gave his daughter, Elizabeth I, was to build shipyards. He told her, "We need the greatest navy in the world to conquer the world." For 300 years, England basically ruled the globe. Over that period of time, England had colonies from India to Australia to North America, all the way around. The sun never set on the British Empire.

One of the biggest ports then was in Lancashire. A lot of British sailors came out of this area because when ships lost men at sea, they would shanghai men—take them on board forcibly and only untie them after getting out to sea—and a lot of those shanghaied happened to be Lancashire wrestlers. So they went around the world—not because they wanted to, because they had to. They saw things around the world, picked up all different holds and tried different wrestling styles, brought them back to Lancashire, and Lancashire catch wrestlers improved on these holds, figured out how they could blend them into their style, and that's how catch-as-catch-can was formed.

It's like the way that modern day MMA has improved so much over the last 10 years. Just 10 years ago, watching MMA was like watching amateur street fighters. Now it's improved because guys who are very good with different styles have come into it, and they've taught from each other. But even the best of MMA can't compare with a mediocre catch wrestler of the 1930s or earlier. I think that's because back then there were just so many more catch wrestlers. You had catch wrestlers all around the world—thousands upon thousands of them. You could go to any city in the world and find dozens of people to spar with. In the mid-1800s through to the early 1900s, working-class guys were working round the clock on eight-hour shifts, so gyms were full 24 hours a day. After their shift was over, they'd get something to eat and go to the gym and find different sparring partners. Practice was never difficult.

There were other styles, too, in England. For example, the Cornish Devonshire style was brought to England in 1066 by William the Conqueror and the Normans. Most of these Normans later settled in Cornwall. The wrestlers wore jackets like a judo jacket, and the style had takedowns, great standing throws, submissions, and chokes. It was similar to judo, and in the early '50s, in fact, the Japanese Judo Championship navy team visited England and entered the Cornish-style wrestling championships. Not one of them got through the first round. They were all thrown or submitted or beaten.

Comparing the English styles of wrestling—Cornish, catch-as-catch-can, and Cumberland Westmorland—is like comparing the Eastern styles of judo, jiu-jitsu, and karate. The three English styles are basically from the same country, but without doubt catch wrestling is the best because it is freer, more open. Matches used to have longer time periods than we see today in any kind of fighting; the basic rules of catch-as-catch-can wrestling included pinfalls and submissions (any kind: leg submissions, neck submissions, and so on), but specifics were argued between the managers of the two sides.

Participant weight was the first thing managers would argue about. If one guy was a lot bigger than the other, his opponent's manager would try to get him to drop weight to make him weaker for the match. In a long match, or an hour match, that would just drain the energy out of him.

Then they would argue about the rules. In straight catch, everything, including all submissions, was allowed. Only fists were forbidden, because most of these guys had day jobs, and when you use fists, you can break a knuckle or a thumb, which would put you out of work. So the heel of the hand, which is solid bone, was allowed. Elbows were allowed. Jumps were allowed. Chokes were sometimes allowed, depending on the agreement. "All in catch" meant everything was allowed—chokes, sleeper holds, everything.

Today, nobody—no amateur, no so-called catch wrestler—really knows how to put the legs in for ankle submission rides. Some of the old-time leg wrestlers were just unbelievable. They could get figure-four body scissors, and they'd squeeze their opponent, tightening up in time with their breathing, like a boa constrictor. If, for example, Joe Robinson got a figure four on you, he'd control your breathing. When you breathed out, he'd tighten and cinch up a little, so you couldn't get enough oxygen. You'd be gasping just to get air, while he'd be working constantly with a side headlock, back elbow, cross-face, or whatever.

In an hour match, the leg wrestlers would be down with all their weight arched out on their opponent, putting a body scissors or figure four scissors on their opponent, and they'd have their hands free, hitting the opponent with the heel of their hands and with their elbow. That opponent's going to fight like hell to free himself, burning out in no time.

The great thing about pinfalls is that the opponent is fighting off his back to get into a defence position so he can sit out, stand up, or counter. As he tries to get to that safe haven position, there will be exposed ankles, loose arms, loose wrists, an opening for a neck crank; whatever comes available can be used to beat him—and that's when the old-timers picked their submissions. It's a lot easier to get submissions when a guy is fighting to get off his back than if he is on his back more passively, like the guard you see in Gracie jiu-jitsu. Pinning opens up doors to so many different things.

The catch guys were beating a lot of the old jiu-jitsu guys, so they changed the rules to no ankle submissions and no neck cranks, to give them a chance. The rules and the time limits have changed so much that now it's mostly just about power. The longest amateur wrestling match, held at the 1912 Olympics, lasted 11 hours and 40 minutes. After that, they made the time limit one hour, and in my time as an amateur it was

15 minutes—six, three, three, three. You start with six minutes standing, then three minutes defence on the mat, followed by three minutes in the attack position on top of the mat. If nobody has been pinned by then, whoever is ahead on points can decide the position he wants to be in to start the last three minutes. So you had to know all aspects of wrestling to be a champion. Nowadays, a championship match is three five-minute rounds or five five-minute rounds.

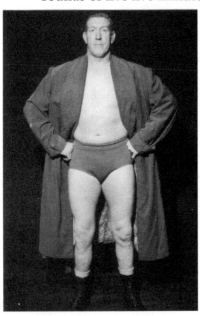

In Billy's opinion, the very best wrestler of his time Billy Joyce (a.k.a. Bob Robinson).

Amateur wrestling is nothing like what it was in the '20s and the '30s. Today, nobody knows breakdowns. Right now, if you can get behind a guy, you get a takedown or get a go-behind, that's it. All you've got to do is stay in there for the end of the round, or you can let him escape. You get two points; he gets one point. That's boring! I don't even watch the Olympics now.

In catch-as-catch-can, there are no points. It's a cat-and-mouse game. It's not about power; the old-timers, like Billy Joyce and those other guys, never got tired on the mat. They could stay on the mat for three, four hours. When I was training for matches, Billy would bring in five or six guys for me. He'd send them in one after another for three minutes or five minutes and change off. For hours, I'd never come off the mat. But I wouldn't get tired. Billy Joyce, John Foley, Jack Dempsey, Joe Carroll, Charlie Carroll—those guys never got tired. When you know how to wrestle, you make the other person do all the work.

If you know the alignment from the ball of the foot to the ankle to the knee to the hip, and how to get power for your leg just from the ankle, you use strength from your body structure, not your muscles. Power is directed from the ball of the foot to the heel and straight up to the knee, and where your heel and your knee are going, that's the direction of your power.

THE GYM CULTURE

A lot of people are familiar with Riley's gym because of people like Karl Gotch and me, but there are so many names that have been totally forgotten, that people don't have any idea about. The history is lost forever.

Billy Riley started in Pop Charnock's gym. Charnock was a world champion before Billy. Then they split and hated each other. Whether it was something personal or it was just the question of who was the better wrestler, I will never know, because I wasn't in a position to ask. In those days, if you said something wrong, it was a slap over the ear and somebody would be grinding you through the mat. You were very careful what you said to Mr. Riley.

Pop Charnock's and Billy Riley's gyms were not the only gyms then. There were plenty of others—Emil Foy, Jimmy Nibletts, and Foley each had their own. Foley was from Leigh, but he had learned with Billy. I started my own gym later, too. And these were just a few of the gyms around Wigan in my time. It was the same all around the world, though mostly in boxing. You could go to any city and there'd be many boxing gyms—people wanted to make money to make life easier, and anybody who was any good at fighting made money privately in street fights, or turned pro.

In those days, every gym had its own deal, and anybody could come into a gym to spar. The guys there would cut out all their top-of-the-line stuff and just do good basic wrestling, get a good workout. They didn't want to teach anybody their top-class stuff in case they had to wrestle competitively in the future. If a visitor asked how he'd been beaten, they would say something like, "Oh, I was lucky. I don't really know what I did." Or if the visitor wanted to see something they did while they were sparring, they'd show him, but not the correct way.

No gym ever really taught an outsider. The basics and may be a few other things, but nothing that could be used to beat them in the future. It was the same way all around the world. If you wanted to learn Gusti, the Indian style of wrestling, you could go to the different gyms in India, like the gyms of the Great Gama and the Bholu Brothers (Gama's nephews), who were world famous. All the gyms in India were the same. You worked out either very early in the morning or very late, after the sun had gone down, because you're in a Quonset hut and you wrestle in sand, and it's very hot during the daytime. In Lancashire, a lot of the matches, or what Americans called "shoots,"

were done on grass—not nice, soft grass like on a bowling green, but more like the turf on a rugby or soccer field. That's why you'd see all the old-timers wearing tights and boots or knee pads, to protect them from grass burns. In a long match, boy, those could go bad on you.

In India, if you were visiting a gym and wanted to learn one hold, you could buy that hold, and they'd teach you it but nothing more. You'd get every aspect of how

After Billy's first match in Japan; he beat Rasha Kimura. Billy is wearing the British Heavyweight Championship belt.

27

to get the hold and the defences against it. Then you were out; they'd show you nothing else. There were no fight photos or video footage then, and you never saw what else they could do.

It was only after the Second World War and the affluence of the '50s that television got it all out into the open. Videos and television changed combat sports tremendously. Nowadays, you can scout a fighter. You can watch all of your opponent's matches before you get on the mat with him. In those days, you never saw your opponent until the match started. That's why jiu-jitsu guys never did any good against catch wrestlers. They picked up things like figure four scissors, which they called the triangle, or a double wristlock, which they renamed the Kimura because he beat them with it. Kimura learned it from Karl Gotch, and Gotch learned it in Wigan with Joe Robinson and Billy Riley. Double wristlocks were around for over a thousand years. But Kimura beat the Gracies, so they named it a Kimura.

What happens is young people watch what the current champions are winning with. Then they copy it, even try to better it, but it's the same hold or moves. They forget a lot of other stuff that's won other matches. Then maybe 30 years go by. One of those forgotten holds comes up again, and a champion starts to beat everybody with it. So everybody wants to learn it. It's a cycle. For example, at the 1948 Olympics in London, the Turks did very well with the top ride, and people started calling it the Turkish ride. Everybody was talking about the Turkish ride that won so many medals in the 1948 games. So I went to Billy Riley, and I said, "Mr Riley, everybody is talking about the Turkish ride."

Billy said, "Well, what is it?" So I described it to him.

He said, "Come in here." Riley's office was a library of wrestling books and prints. He brought out etchings that were 400 or 500 years old of exactly the same ride, and he said, "The Turkish ride? We were doing that over 500 years ago."

Billy Riley sent me to different gyms to wrestle their guys and come back and tell him what I had a problem with or what was tough. He had other guys there from our gym watching; I didn't know it then. He sent old-timers that I didn't know to see what I needed to work on, what I was doing wrong, and so on. He knew before I came back to tell him.

Riley sent me not only to the local gyms, but to other countries. He sent me to Germany to work out with Gideon Gida, the Hungarian Greco-Roman champion. Gida had improved Karl Gotch's suplex. Karl was already very good with the suplex, but Gida coached him to make it even better. Later, Gida and Karl became very close friends. Gida was like an uncle to me. He was very close to my family, to Alf and my dad. He was great. He showed me the double arm suplex that I beat everybody with later in my career.

Gideon Gida, Greco-Roman champion, with Billy's son Spencer.

When I asked him how he had figured it out, he said, "Well, I didn't. A very good friend of mine won the silver medal in the Greco with that hold in the '36 Olympic games. He was from Germany. His name was Wolfgang Ehrl, a.k.a. Bubby Ehrl. 'Bubby' means little boy in German, and that was his nickname."

Gida wrestled in a tournament in Munich, and I went with him, and Bubby was a postmaster for Munich at that time. Gida introduced us. Bubby showed me the hold. Then we went to the gym and worked on it together every day for about a week—how to get into it, how to get submissions from it, and how to defend it.

AT RILEY'S

Billy Riley is the best coach I've ever been around. He didn't teach me just wrestling. He didn't teach me only catch-as-catch-can. He taught me how to learn. He taught me to open my mind to angles, to the metrics, to the alignments of the ankle, the hip, the elbows, the shoulders. He explained how my body worked, how I could get the most power out of my body, how I could save energy and still make my opponent think I was the strongest man he'd ever been on the mat with; he taught me how to break their heart.

So much of catch-as-catch-can is wearing a man out and knowing how to break his spirit. For example, I get a good escape guy, and I keep taking him down. And then I let him fight up, but only three-quarters of the way up, and then I take him down again. While making it easy for him to get three-quarters of the way up, I'm setting myself in a position so that he will go down floundering again, using a lot of energy. This is what Bob Robinson, a.k.a. Billy Joyce, did so well.

The first time I went on the mat with Bob all the old-timers were there. I had been going for a year, and I hadn't been on the mat with any of the top men. Bob had an appointment for a private match. He was getting ready, and he wanted somebody to train with. Riley said, "Okay, Billy, get on the mat with him." So I get up to wrestle Bob after he's worked out with all these other guys, and everybody's gone except the old-timers. Bob takes me down, half-halches me, plays with me a bit, takes me down again, and then lets me get halfway up. While I am half bent over, I notice that his weight is entirely on his heel and that he has taken his toes completely off the mat.

Now I'm on one knee on the mat, and with his toes in the air, I'm thinking about going underneath, grabbing his foot, and getting an ankle lock roll to finish with an ankle submission. As I put my hand underneath, he just changes his weight on top of my hand. Now I can't get the hand out. All the old-timers are laughing hard. He then just turns me over like nothing, gets a top wrist-lock on the other arm, and makes me submit. I get up. I say, "Bob, you tricked me that time." One of the old-timers said, "Yeah and he's going to trick you a few more times before you get done." That's how it was back then.

Syed Said Shah was one of the great Gusti wrestlers from India. He wrestled an hour draw with Goga, one of the Gama's nephews, and he was going to wrestle Bob. They were promoting, and Shah was saying, "I can get anybody's leg." Well, everyone told him he couldn't get Bob's leg. So they get into the ring, and straight away Shah goes for the leg. Bob moves the leg out of the way. He stuck his leg in front of him again and pulled it away about three or four times. Each time he did it, he slowed down taking his leg out of the way. So, about the fifth time, Shah was going for the leg and his fingertips got about two inches from Bob's knee. Bob took his knee back at the same speed as Shah's arm so Shah still thought he could get him, until he had overreached. Then Bob just plopped him over and made him submit with a wristlock.

Bob Robinson was both British and European heavyweight champion, and many experts thought him to be the best technical wrestler of all time. He had long string-bean arms, his hands hung lower than his knees, and he had big thighs but no calves. He was one of the nicest guys around. He wouldn't even swear. In England, "fucking hell" was a common expression among the working-class people; he wouldn't even say that. If he really got mad at something, he'd just take a few deep breaths and stutter out, "kin' hell!" That was the closest he'd get to swearing. He was very quiet-spoken. In a bar or out on the street, he'd be a real mark for some of these guys who thought they were tough. Bob could beat a person so fast without using any energy; he was just unbelievably good.

Let me tell you about Jimmy Hart, the nicest guy in the world. He had only basic takedowns, but he was a good control artist, a very good leg rider; he'd hook his opponent with one leg deep, hook the ankle with the other, get a scissors on the other ankle, and squeeze the knees together. It's what we call the top ride. It would only take him about a minute to get me down and get his legs in. He'd cross-face me one way,

"The Last Traditional Wrestler of Catch-As-Catch-Can style"

Billy Robinson (Wigan)

slip the elbow over my head, then back-elbow my head all the way back. My spine and neck would go click, click, click, click, click, until he couldn't go any farther, and then he'd slip the back elbow over, cross-face me again, and do it the other way. If I was on the mat an hour, this torture lasted an hour. All I could hear him say was "Never mind, lad; you'll have an 18-inch neck before you're 16 years old," and those were my Friday nights. Back then, I used to catch the train home. I'd have to walk about a quarter of a mile up a steep hill to the bus stop to go to Ashton on the other side of Manchester. I'd have to stop five or six times on those Friday nights just to lean against the wall to rest my neck. It was that beat up.

But that isn't the worst train story I have from those days. Billy Riley uesd to pick me up at the train station and tell me what he wanted me to work on that day. I'm like six-foot-two, 191, and in great shape. Well, I'm walking up the street from or to the station with this 72-year-old guy, and he's grabbing me from behind or hooking or grapevining a leg and reaching around my face. And then, as if that wasn't bad enough, the Irishman in him would have him singing all these old songs, like, "Whatever did Robinson Crusoe do with Friday on Saturday night? Where there are wild men, there have got to be wild women, so what did Robinson Crusoe do with Friday on . . ." I mean, I'll never forget it, because every time we went to the station, after he had finished mauling me, he'd be singing this song for more mortification, until people stopped and stared at us like we were homosexuals. It was so embarrassing! Mind you, homosexuality in those days was against the law in England. This was around the

Billy at 17 after having won the British nationals.

time when Lord Montagu did time in prison for it, even though he was the queen of England's first cousin.

There were so many great wrestlers at Riley's gym—Billy Joyce, Joe Robinson, the Carroll brothers, George Gregory, Mel Ryss, Tommy Moore, John Foley, Ernie Riley (Billy's son), and of course Karl Gotch (Karl Istaz). Karl was a generation ahead of me; he was in the 1948 Olympics, and I won the 1957 Nationals. After the Olympics in 1948, Karl turned pro in Belgium. My uncle Alf went to Antwerp to wrestle Jack Sherry for the World Championship. Karl was on the same card. They started talking about Wigan and submission wrestling, and Karl didn't believe it. Alf invited him over. So Karl came and stayed at our house when I was a young kid.

And when Karl went to Wigan, it was exactly the same as when I went to Wigan a few years later. The guys at the gym played exactly the same thing. Karl looked at Dempsey and Foley, then Billy Joyce and George Gregory; he thought they were too small or too old. After a short while, they had all beaten him easily. George and Billy played with him. Remember that Karl hadn't learned submissions or catch-as-catch-can yet. He was just a very good amateur wrestler. "That's it," Karl said; he didn't even go back to Belgium. He lived in Wigan for the next six or seven years.

I first met Karl when I was 10 or 11 years old. And then I sparred with him. He needed sparring partners, and I was the only guy who turned up. Anyway, he beat me very easily. He made me submit, but I kept on coming back. He was getting pissed, but I wasn't going to quit, not with my dad watching. When I say "quit," I mean I wasn't tired, so I didn't want to stop, no matter how hard it was. Afterwards, I had to take three days off work because of the abuse to my body.

One of the toughest and best matches I've ever seen was a supposedly friendly workout between Foley and Dempsey. It was unbelievable—great technique, great moves, and hard. They got black eyes, their noses were bent, there was blood coming out of their ears and mouth, and they were still the best of friends afterwards. But neither would give up; nobody was going to bow down to anybody.

There was a certain attitude at the gym—a lot of

camaraderie, even pranks. For instance, there were copper heating pipes going around the gym. They'd get red hot. They had to, because the gym was so cold. With the English weather, no matter how much heat you've got, it's still cold because of the dampness. Well, it was very cold on this particular day, so we lit the gas heater. It took a while for the gym to warm up, but the copper pipes got hot fast. We went in to spar, and I tied up with Bob Robinson. He must have winked, because I could see everybody hitting their elbows and smiling. They knew something was about to happen.

Though I knew something was going on, I couldn't figure out what. Robinson made me move in such a way that my backside hit the pipes, and those pipes were red hot! I screamed and jumped; as I did, he sent me through the air and made me hit the mat hard. Everybody was laughing. "He's tricked you again, kid."

They did a lot of stuff like that. When it was a match between a great guy and a beginner, they'd pull tricks on the beginner, but only if they respected him. When it was two of the best guys coming up, it was like two pit bulls going at each other.

One time, one of the wrestlers, Billy Howes, had just come back from the Korean War and had just started to work out at Wigan again. What he did was he wired the end of the big steel barbell in the gym to this machine, where you couldn't see the wires, and when someone picked up the bar, he'd turn it on, and

Alf executing a hype on a young Billy Robinson.

they couldn't let go of it because of the DC current. He caught me and almost everybody else with it.

Then one day, Billy Riley and Ernie Riley came in because Billy was going to watch Ernie and me work out. Now, Billy Riley and Joe Robinson had a competitive relationship, even in their older days. Billy Riley didn't show Karl a lot, but that's probably a big part of why Joe showed Karl what he did about catch-as-catch-can. That day at the gym, the old-timers at the gym started talking about Joe. So Billy Howes said, "We just watched Joe. He was in here earlier with some other group of guys. He picked that weight up, and when he got it to his chest, he pressed it, and his arms moved so slowly, you could hardly see the weight moving up. Can you do that, Billy?"

"If Joe can do it, I can do it," Billy Riley said. Off came his muffler, his jacket, and his cap. He pulled his shirtsleeves up, and as he went to pick the weight up, they turned the DC current on. Everybody's laughing, but what happened was Billy Howes had turned the electricity up too much, so Billy Riley's body started shaking. Ernie grabbed his dad to pull him off, but because of the electrical current, now Ernie's stuck to the back of his dad trying to pull him off. It was like two dogs humping each other.

So Billy Howe yelled to me, "Billy, I'm out of here. When I get out of that door, turn it off." So he ran out, and I turned it off. Nobody was hurt, and there was no ill feeling. It was just hilarious.

We used to have guys there who were very good gym wrestlers but would never make it with the real top catch wrestlers. They were still very dangerous in the gym. Outside it, wrestling in another gym or in a match somewhere, it didn't work for them, for some unknown reason; but in their own gym, they were good. They were part of the family. They were great sparring partners because they wouldn't quit. They knew really good basics, and they were better than 90 percent of everyone else out there. Everybody loved them because we could practise our stuff with them.

If they ever got in trouble on the street or anything, and you were there, it was like protecting your own family. There was no stabbing in the back, no bullshitting. I never learned anything about that sort of thing until I came to America.

American pro wrestling changed a lot of things for me. The attitude was different. Nowadays, a lot of the younger wrestlers expect encouragement from their coaches. Billy Riley never said anything, not after I won the European Championship, or any amateur championships for that matter. Even when I beat Bob Robinson for the British Heavyweight Championship, Riley never gave me one good word. Finally, when I won the World Championships, he said, "That was good."

I started to reply, "Mr. Riley . . ."

He stopped me and said, "You can call me Billy now."

I said, "Billy, thank you. All the time that I've spent with you, all these years, all the time—three, four, sometimes five times a week, you never said 'good' to me once. When I beat the Olympic team from Sweden, when I beat someone in a private match, you never said a good word."

He said, "It's not my place to tell you what's good. I'm here to tell you what's wrong and teach you how to fix it. Plus, once you start to believe you're good, you'll stop learning." He really taught me to keep an open mind.

I sparred with a lot of the old-timers. No matter what time of the day it was, there were always old-timers, really great old catch-as-catch-can wrestlers, at the gym. And they'd watch all the young guys wrestling. Some would take a liking to one kid or another, and they'd pull them to one side after the match, or after their sparring session, and say, "Listen, when you do this, if you just change your angle just a little bit here and then drop your hip and get the alignment of your knee and your ankle, you'll find that you will feel a lot stronger. Now, try it again."

The big difference nowadays is people want to learn the finishing holds before they learn how to wrestle. The idea of catch wrestling is to know how you can get the finishing hold from whatever position you're in, not to just go after it openly so your opponent knows what you're trying to do. Billy used to scream at me, "Don't telegraph what you are going to do."

For example, when I cross-face, when I'm turning my opponent's head, he thinks I'm trying to make him submit with a neck crank, and he's trying to defend it. But I'm actually pulling him right onto his own ankle. I change suddenly and get the ankle submission from him. Today, a lot of the so-called catch wrestlers and ankle submission guys think they know it all. Sure, ankle submission's a great submission, but you'd *never* get in that position with a guy that knows catch wrestling.

In 1956, my first year at the nationals, I came in

Billy's signature move: the double arm suplex.

third. And then, the following year, 1957, I won the nationals in amateur wrestling. Later that year, there was the European Open Championships in Ireland, and I wrestled in two weight classes. In light heavyweight, I beat the fourth-place finisher at the 1956 Olympics, Gerry Martina. Then, in heavyweight, Ken Richmond, the bronze medallist at the 1952 Olympics, beat me. I wrestled Richmond about a month later at the YMCA and beat him that time. I was a little bit in awe of him when we first wrestled, which Billy Riley chewed me out for. He said to me, "Listen, son, you've won all the cups and the medals. Why don't you take me out? I taught you how to wrestle. Take me out and buy me a steak dinner?"

I said, "Mr. Riley, I'd love to, but I can't afford to take you out and buy you a steak dinner."

He said, "It just goes to show you, kid. You can't buy steaks with medals. It's time you turned pro." And he was right; with all the television and the coverage coming in a little bit later, it was a good choice for me. The only thing I really regret is that I didn't wait to go to the Olympics. I should have gone. I had beaten everyone who went as part of the British team.

The last three years at Riley's gym, I was pro wrestling and going to different countries. Eventually, I ended up opening my own gym in Manchester, which was a Lancashire-style catch gym, the same as Billy Riley's. I was teaching people what Billy taught me.

CHAPTER THREE
WRESTLING THE WORLD OVER

Turning pro at nineteen was great for me because it allowed me to travel. It was the time when the great Hungarian amateur wrestlers in Germany—Gideon Gida, Josef Kovacs, Joe Mulnar, Michael Nadar, Tibor Szakacs, Peter Szakacs—wanted to take pro wrestling into Sweden. There was no pro wrestling in Sweden in those days, so the Swedish Olympic team said, "No, you've got to show us how good you are and beat us first." Gida called me to help out. Now, Gida had helped me a lot with the Greco and the suplex. He was like family. Though I was originally supposed to go to Japan to help Yoshimura, I couldn't refuse Gida. So I went to Sweden.

There, I wrestled with Axel Grönberg, who was

a two-time Olympic champion and world champion. I also beat Gösta Andersson, who was an Olympic champion. I beat them all at amateur. Then I beat Andersson with submission wrestling because he quit after a minute and said, "Hey, it's too dangerous for us." So that's how we got pro wrestling into Sweden; it was brought in by the Hungarian amateurs and by a Wigan catch wrestler (that is, me) beating their champions.

I began travelling all about. I had gone to school with a guy who was now a pro wrestler, a very well-educated kid, and he was friends with a promoter in Spain, an opposition promoter called Jesus Chausson. He offered me twice as much money as I was earning in England to go to Spain and wrestle, but unfortunately, in England, Joint Promotions were all united, and if you wrestled for an opposition promoter, you were out. So Billy Riley called me and said, "Billy, you can't go there and wrestle for Jesus Chausson, otherwise you won't wrestle for Joint Promotions again or for the big promoters in Europe."

I said, "Mr Riley, I've got to go. I gave my word." That was my first disagreement with Billy Riley.

So I went to Spain, and when I got there, nobody was there to meet me! What had happened was that Chausson had packed up his business, so I was left in Madrid with very little money in my pocket and nowhere to go. (Incidentally, about a year later, I had a match with Jesus Chausson in London, and I was still pissed. I gave him nothing; I was all over him. It must have been a boring match to watch for the public, with me just abusing him the whole time. I remember, at one point, I heard a voice with a Cockney accent cry out from the crowd, "Come on, Jesus, for Christ's sake!" The whole audience broke into laughter.)

Fortunately, an American English professor who was teaching at the University of Madrid had sat next to me on the plane. He said, "Come and stay with me for a couple of days until we get you sorted out." So I spent a week with him. Then he got me into very cheap hotel lodgings. He also got me a job as a Roman soldier in the movie *King of Kings*. Being a wrestler and in good shape, and speaking English, I had no problem getting the job. There, I met Sophia Loren and Charlton Heston. They weren't in that movie, but they came on the set to visit, and I was introduced because I was a wrestler. She was the most beautiful thing I had ever seen in those days.

The English professor also introduced me to Ernest Hemingway. The professor and me, we went to the bullfights one afternoon, and Hemingway was there. We got talking because he liked to box and spar. We talked about wrestling, my uncle, and my father. Later that night, he even came to the wrestling matches to watch me fight. I had a great day with him, though I didn't realize his importance then. I read his books after that point; he was a great guy, and he was a big man, a big, barrel-chested man. I don't know if he was six feet, but he reminded me of my father, with that big barrel chest.

One day, the English professor called me. He said, "Billy, your name is in the newspapers." At the Plaza de Toros, the big bull arena in Madrid, they put a ring in the center of the bullring on Sundays and had pro wrestling after the bullfights. I was the semi-main event there, so I called the promoter. I said, "Excuse me, are you using my name?"

He said, "Yes. As you didn't wrestle for Jesus Chausson and you haven't been against Joint Promotions, we'll take you in. Come down to the office, and we'll talk money." I went and talked money and spent two summers in Spain, 1960 and 1961. I had a great time there.

Pro wrestling in a lot of countries is a seasonal event. In England, it's year-round. In Belgium and France, it's year-round. But in Germany, Spain, and Austria, it is just in the summer. So in the summers, I'd go to tournaments in Spain, doing single matches in all the major cities.

After Spain, I came back to England and then went to the German tournaments in 1961. People were starting to talk about how I was from Wigan and how good I was. Now, I was good as an English amateur, a British amateur champion, but compared to the top catch wrestlers, I wasn't really that good in those days. I understood that because it was driven into me, regularly. Every time I won something or beat somebody,

I hated going back to the gym the next day, because I knew what would happen. I wouldn't be sparring with somebody who should be able to beat me. I would be sparring with an old-timer who I was a lot bigger than, a lot younger than, a lot stronger than. And he'd beat the living shit out of me.

The cross-body suplex.

I was starting to improve, though, because I was getting more experience competing with the top wrestlers of different countries. I ran into a lot of good wrestlers—Ivan Martinson from France; Spanish guys like Jose Arroyo and Pedro Bengochea, the Spanish champion in those days. I wrestled everybody of note in Europe.

In Germany, I wrestled Peter Kaiser, who was Gustl Kaiser's nephew and the German amateur champion, in a private training session. He said, "Come on. I want to see how good you can wrestle." I pinned or submitted him 13 times, and he pinned me once. Josef Kovacs was there, and since I beat Peter easily, I had to wrestle him that night, too.

Kovacs was trying to show me how good he was, but he didn't quite get away with it. We finished up wrestling a draw, a 20-minute draw, because that's what the matches were in Germany—five four-minute rounds. Further on in the tournament, it would go to 30-minute matches, and then the final would be six ten-minute rounds.

I remember Gustl Kaiser used to go into a big speech every night about his athletes, his "gladiators." He'd challenge anybody to come down and work out if they wanted to try, and they could pick anybody they wanted out of the tournament to work out with. This was the year before I won my first tournament. It was great for me, a great learning experience. I loved it. I was beating these guys who thought they were so tough. They were street fighters, mostly. Some of them did know how to wrestle, too, and there were judo and karate guys. Oddly, the judo and karate guys were the easiest to beat *because they had discipline.* A street fighter had no discipline, so it was difficult to size up what they were going to do just by looking at where their body was going. They'd kick from the wrong angle or throw a punch from the wrong angle, and if you were not aware, they'd catch you, so it was a good learning experience for me.

Normally, in a two- or three-week tournament, you'd get all the guys from the dock areas who thought themselves tough. Maybe two or three would come down during a three-week tournament—one a week or so. This tournament was no different. Then something odd started to happen. Every day at the tournament, there were two or three guys who wanted to train with me. They didn't want to train with anybody else. At the next tournament, it was the same thing. It was odd!

What had happened was Geoff Portz, another English wrestler and a very good friend of mine, was going out to the toughest bars in the roughest areas in all these different towns, saying, "Billy Robinson thinks all you guys are Nazis. Nazis are bullies, and all bullies are cowards." Now, it's true that I felt bullies were cowards. It was a thing that I picked up from my father—if anybody was a bully, don't worry about him, because if you faced him, he'd back down. If he knocked you down five times, get up again, and he'd quit on you. Anyway, Geoff was challenging all these guys, every night, and I didn't know about it. When I finally found out at the last tournament of the season,

The double arm suplex.

I chased him up and down the different aisles of the Circus Krone arena in Munich. I couldn't catch him, and everybody was laughing because they knew what he had done. Guys would pull tricks like that, but they'd watch your back, too, which was great about wrestling.

After Germany, I went to Belgium, because my uncle wrestled over there. He was a big name there, having fought American Jack Sherry, the world champion at that time. Karl Gotch was from Antwerp, Belgium, a country that had some good catch wrestlers. Not as good as the Wigan guys, but still pretty tough. The promoter would book us for two weeks at a time or a week at a time, and we'd go to Antwerp and up into the different towns in Belgium and France, because it was right on the French border where they promoted.

In Belgium, you've basically got two languages—one half of Belgium speaks French, and the other half speaks Flemish, which is like what Germans used to speak 300 years ago. The people from Antwerp who spoke Flemish wouldn't speak French to the people from the French part of Brussels, and vice versa. They used English with each other. Neither would back down and speak the other's language.

I loved Antwerp, especially the zoo. The King of Belgium loved gorillas, so the zoo had a special section for them; it was unbelievable! There were no bars or cages. It was all glass, and this was 1962, when all the great zoos in the world had cages, not glass. You could walk in and see all kinds of gorillas—from the big lowland and highland gorillas to the silverbacks. Everything inside the area was wired up to an electric scale outside so that if they hit or grabbed or squeezed something, the scale would show the pressure they could generate. I could spend all day there just watching the gorillas.

In France, I had a lot of challenge private matches—guys who thought they were tough or guys who wanted to show what they could do. Maybe because I'm English, I didn't like France that much. It used to be pretty dirty, unlike Germany, Austria, and Switzerland, which were very clean countries. Pigalle and other areas of France were fun to have a night out. Nice, in the south of France, and those areas towards Spain—Provence and Normandy, they were different. They had a lot of well-educated people with big yachts and money. It was a completely different atmosphere.

The French also invented a lot of champions. They'd call the French heavyweight champions the world champions, but anytime one of them got into trouble, they'd send to Wigan—to Dempsey, Foley, the Belshaw brothers, or to Billy Joyce—to come over and take care of the problem for them.

One country that I loved visiting was Lebanon. When I was visiting, there were no wars there. From Arabia to Iran to Iraq, big oil countries were all around Lebanon, and it was the oil sheiks' playground. You had casinos like in Vegas. You had beaches like in Hawaii. You could go out a quarter of a mile into the Mediterranean and see the bottom of the ocean. The ocean was that clean. Surfing, swimming, everything was there. As far as cuisine went, Lebanon was where the East met the West; there were so many great restaurants. The weather was fantastic.

As a history buff, I loved Lebanon. If you went 30 miles down the coast, you'd reach Byblos, where Richard the Lionheart landed during the Third Crusade. He built a castle around Byblos, and that's where he started his crusade to take Jerusalem back. Around 1908, some guy going through the desert tripped over what seemed to be a piece of rock in the sand. He started to dig, and out came the entire Roman city of Baalbek. They cleaned it out, and there was the arena along with other beautiful buildings. Starting in 1955, all the greatest musicians and dancers have come to Baalbek every year to perform at the old coliseum for the International Festival. I saw Nureyev and Fontaine dance there, and I listened to different orchestras. It was just beautiful. They would put me in for one match, and every time, I'd stay a couple of weeks and visit Baalbek and Byblos, looking at the places where the gladiators lived, fought, and died.

After the first war with Israel, things changed. But before that, if you went down the main street of Beirut, there would be something like three Mercedes taxis, a Rolls-Royce, four camels, and then a donkey and cart. It was a mixture of the East and West, of money and poverty. Everything was there. I had a friend in Lebanon, Ray Joseph, a.k.a. Ray Apollon, from Trinidad. His father was a very famous doctor. He went to school in Paris, but he got into pro wrestling and spent his money on it instead of going to the University of Paris. He was a big black man with great weightlifting strength. We became very good friends.

In 1962, I went to India, and on the way back I stopped in Lebanon. Ray was wrestling, and his cousin Al Rodagua was there. Al was from Venezuela. He was having a private match with some guy in Lebanon, so Ray asked me if I could work out with him. So every morning I would go to the gym when I really wanted

In Trinidad with Ray Apollon and a fan.

to be on the beaches looking at all these beautiful girls from England and Paris. They were there because the oil millionaires were feeding them money just to be around them. It was gorgeous!

One day, there's this big guy standing with his arms folded, saying, *"Pas possible, pas possible,"* whenever I showed Rodagua different things to do. I was getting pissed off at him. He was a lot bigger than I was—about 70 or 80 pounds heavier, though probably my height—and he was on the Olympic team for Greco-Roman and freestyle. I went over to Ray and asked, "What's going on?"

Ray said, "Oh, he's just saying that what you are showing can't be done with him. He'd beat you easily from it."

I said, "Okay, tell him to come on the mat and let him show me. A little bit into it, I'm going to wink at you, and I want you to just say, 'Billy, stop playing around and finish it.'"

As soon as we came to hook up with each other, I hooked his bottom rib with the heel of my hand and put my elbow in my body and just walked him right off the mat. Well, he was so much bigger than me, so he got really embarrassed. He tried to do the same thing to me, but I wouldn't let him. I kept on slipping to the side, bobbing and getting a single, trying to go behind him. I didn't really want to go behind him. I wanted to give him the chance to come straight at me.

So once I got him set up straight on the mat, I

winked at Ray. He said, "Okay, Billy, stop playing around." I went in to push him again, and he drove forward, of course. I popped his elbow up, dropped down my knees, grabbed his heel, and hit his kneecap with my other shoulder. But his body weight was so far over that, when I hit the knee, his body weight couldn't get back in time, and the knee joint snapped. His leg was bent the wrong way at a 45-degree angle. He went to the hospital.

The next day, after I'd been working out with Al Rodagua again, I was swimming in the pool. The big guy was there with a cast on his leg, and there were some other guys around. They were all multimillionaires who were backing the guy for the Olympics. I got introduced to all these guys, and they took me out to all the different casinos. We became friends. But that two-week visit was the only time I met him, because the war broke out not too much later. I remember I was on the beach in Beirut, and the police came over to take me back to the hotel. I thought I had done something wrong. I didn't know they were just getting me out because they knew the war was coming in only two days; I got my ticket on the plane.

I was very lucky. My father always said, "Billy, when you go abroad, forget you're English. You try to understand the language, try to learn the language, try their foods, and try to understand their customs. No matter what country you're in, if the people see you trying, they will help you." That advice has worked for me in every country I've been to.

I had a great experience in India, too. Because India was under the British rule for centuries, the country was very pro-English. The promoter there was Dara Singh, and two guys that I'd wrestled with in England—George Gordienko and John da Silva—were there already. Dara Singh had wanted somebody else from England to come over, and they suggested me.

When I first got there, there was nobody to meet me at the airport in Bombay, so I took a taxi downtown and stayed at the Taj Mahal Hotel, by the Gateway of India. I had told Dara Singh that I wanted a return booking, and if somebody didn't contact me within two days, I was leaving. Because of what I'd learned from my earlier experience in Spain, I'd got my return airfare beforehand. Fortunately, they contacted me within two days.

The ride from the airport to the Taj Mahal Hotel was shocking. I mean, there were dead beasts on the road with carrion birds pecking away at them. People were going around with death carts, picking up bodies and throwing them into the cart. In those days, Bombay and Calcutta each had a million people sleeping on the streets. And if they'd earned enough money that day, they could rent a little bamboo cot to raise them six or eight inches off the roadway so rats would run underneath their bed and wouldn't start nibbling at their toes. I had heard stories about the conditions in India,

Bombay, 1962.

but to see it for the first time was horrible.

Wrestling was a big thing in India. They had their own style of wrestling—Gusti. For a long time, it has been debated whether the Indian clubs and the Indian squats were originally Indian or brought by Persians to India. It's like Muay Thai in Thailand and Savate in France; whether that style of kickboxing originated in Thailand, or in France, or whether the navy people had picked it up somewhere, nobody will ever know.

While in India, I wrestled a top Gusti wrestler who had challenged the visiting pro wrestlers, and I beat him in his own style in about a minute and a half. He was like 360 or 370 pounds. I was about 215 pounds in those days. He stood about six inches taller than me, though the photographs in the newspaper made me look ridiculously small.

I was fortunate enough to wrestle the original

Dara Singh (not the promoter). Now, Dara Singh was a champion equal to all the Bholu brothers and everybody else in his day. But his brother got murdered over a family dispute, and he went and killed three brothers and got put into prison for it.

But his name was so good in wrestling in those days that when Khrushchev visited India, he wanted to see Dara Singh. So they arranged for Singh to have a wrestling match outside the prison. And Khrushchev said to Nehru, "Listen. You shouldn't keep a lion like this imprisoned in a cage." Nehru pardoned Singh. He got out, but he was a lot older then, and I wrestled him in a match and beat him. He was huge, a big, strong guy, but I beat him like I beat a lot of guys—because I was young and coming up while they were old and going out. That happens in wrestling often. It's like Billy Joyce and George Gregory or me and Billy Joyce. When I won the British Championship from Billy Joyce, that was a real match. I mean it wasn't a pro wrestling match. I had to beat him on the level to get the British Championship belt, because that's how you do it in Wigan.

In 1962, when I went to India, there wasn't television there. When we had matches in Bombay, New Delhi, Calcutta, Madras, and other places, wrestlers and promoters would go around the city in rickshaws for two or three days before the matches, and they'd stop every so often to announce through their megaphones: "Ladies and gentlemen, in three days' time, this champion, Billy Robinson, the British Lion, is going to fight Dara Singh, the Indian Lion, at seven o'clock at Cricket Station." That would go on for three days. Now, times are different. You log onto the Internet and see what movie is playing or who is wrestling or who is playing football. Living has become a lot easier.

In India, it was against the law for a Muslim to wrestle or fight with a Hindu, so the Muslim faith inaugurated me to be their champion in India. Consequently, it went over very, very big. While I was there, the beautiful young granddaughter of the Nizam of Hyderabad followed me everywhere I was wrestling, from Bombay to Delhi. She'd be there in the front row of the crowd. We had dinner, and we became very good friends. Now, the Nizam of Hyderabad was the richest man in the world. He owned the Koh-i-noor, once known as the largest diamond in the world. That's the big jewel in the front of Queen Elizabeth's crown.

One of the big deals of knowing the shahzadi (princess) was that I got to go to the Nizam's palace in Hyderabad, and she took me around the museum. In Lebanon, I'd seen where Richard the Lionheart landed on the Third Crusade. As a child, I'd seen Richard the Lionheart's sword in the Tower of London, and now I'm in this museum of the Nizam of Hyderabad, and there's Saladin's sword and all stuff from the Crusades!

Meeting the Governor in Bombay, 1962.

I mean, I'm a 20-year-old that's into the history of England. So that was fantastic.

The Nizam of Hyderabad asked me what I would like to do. I said, "Well, I've always wanted to sail." Two hours later, there's a Rolls-Royce picking me up and taking me to the lake near Hyderabad, and I'm sailing a yacht with a captain teaching me how to tack and everything else.

After India, I went up into Kathmandu, Nepal, and had a great time there. Champions would come over from Persia or the various maharajahs would bring their champions up from India to wrestle, and we wrestled private matches for the king of Nepal. When Dara Singh, Gordienko, and others left Nepal, I stayed there with the American economic advisor to Nepal at that time, one William Tweet. He later became an economics professor at Vanderbilt in Tennessee. I stayed with him and his wife and kids.

While in Nepal, I was introduced to Father Moran from the Catholic school and orphanage, where they have a Billy Robinson Sports Day every year, even to this day! He used to call me "Robinson" all the time, and I absolutely hated it. It came from being raised in England because, with the British military controlling the world for so many hundreds of years, if you addressed a lower-ranked person by their surname, it was a big insult. I mean, you could call somebody a bastard and they would laugh at it, but if you called somebody by their surname, it could very well start a fight. It was Father Moran that got me out of that old custom, and then, being away from England for so long helped, too. I started to coach wrestling in the orphanages there, the very same orphanages that were founded by Hillary and Tenzing, the first people to climb Mount Everest. Tenzing's son, Sherpa Tenzing, was in one of the orphanages.

One day, after coaching, Father Moran asked me to join him for dinner. During the conversation afterward, he asked me to fetch him an open wooden box at the other end of the pool. I went to get it. It was just going dark, and as I neared the box, the hair on the back of my neck stood up. A pair of huge green eyes was staring at me from about 10 feet away. It was a black leopard. For a moment, I thought I was going to be his dinner, until I heard Father Moran chuckling. He assured me that I shouldn't worry, and to just get the box slowly and come back. He told me that the leopard was wild, but that they left food out for him every night in that box, and he left them alone. I was mad, but he was laughing. That was the first time ever that I felt fear.

One time, the Americans in Nepal put on a play about magic called *Bell, Book and Candle* for the king and the Nepalese royal family. Later, it was made into a big movie with James Stewart, Kim Novak, and Jack Lemmon. I was the stage manager for the play. At this time, Bill Tweet introduced me to a person from the German embassy. He was a huge Bavarian and weighed at least 350 pounds. He wanted to finger wrestle. I didn't know what finger wrestling was, but he explained that you interlocked your middle fingers and put your feet so you were standing toe-to-toe, and pulled until one finger straightened out. He beat me quickly. I really had no chance with this guy, and it pissed me off that I let myself get talked into it.

After the play, the royal family had a big ball. The royals had never seen jazz dancing, rock and roll, and the twist. So I danced the twist and the jitterbug. Bill Tweet's wife was a ballerina, so we did a dance where we started off doing the jive and the twist, then the music changed into ballet, and she went into ballet steps and the pirouettes. Toward the end, we had it choreographed in such a way that she'd spin about and her legs would hit into my legs and I'd take a bump. Every time, I'd get up, she'd still be spinning, and I'd take another bump and then another. I had a good time, except that it was hardwood floors, and I'm break-falling like on a wrestling mat. It was hard, but the king enjoyed it so much that he even asked for an encore.

After our dance for the king, the ball turned back to formal dancing, but I've got this big German on my mind. I am still furious and looking for him. I really want to make an example of him because I got really conned into doing the finger-wrestling bit. The next thing I know, somebody's grabbed me from behind around the neck. Well, I'm pissed off thinking about the German, so I turn around and, without looking at his face, do a backbreaker lift. Then, instead of doing the backbreaker, I am going to grab him around the waist, lift him shoulder-high, throw my feet back and do a belly flop. I'd have landed with all my weight on him. In Derby, England, I had beaten a jiu-jitsu guy in a challenge match with this move, and he was knocked out for 25 minutes. Anyway, as I'm picking him up, I realize that whoever it is, they're a lot lighter than 350 pounds.

The music stops, and I see all these Gurkha soldiers taking a step forward, all pulling their kukris out. Gurkhas are very famous Nepalese soldiers, and they have a knife called a kukri. If they draw it from its sheath, they have to draw blood. If they don't get somebody else's blood, they have to cut themselves.

Anyway, I've got the guy up in the air and I look up; it's the king's younger brother. Oh boy, you've never seen *anybody* put down on the floor on his feet so softly in your life. As I gently set him down, he burst out laughing, so then, the Gurkhas retreated and the ballroom dance started again.

I was sweating, though, because earlier that year, a guy had gotten a new truck and he'd accidentally hit a cow and killed it in the middle of the street downtown. People killed him. They hung him from a lamppost because cows were holy for them. In certain areas of the town, rats were holy or monkeys were holy. You could see a stake through a cat in the middle of the street because that cat had killed a rat. If the king's brother had been hurt, it would have turned very bad for me.

When I was in Kathmandu, Prince Carlos of Spain came with his bride, the princess of Greece, on their honeymoon. Franco was still in charge of Spain, and he was setting up Prince

India, 1962.

67

Carlos to become the king. I was invited to the honeymoon party, which was full of dignitaries and ambassadors and different people of note. Prince Carlos was a black belt in judo and enjoyed talking to me about wrestling and judo.

On the way back to England, I returned to Germany. When in India, I had got very ill with jaundice. My eyes went yellow, my skin turned yellow, and I lost a lot of weight. In Germany, Gustl looked at me and said, "Oh, he's too small for my tournament." So a wrestler named Dennis Mitchell said, "Listen, Gustl, I'll wrestle him. Let's see how he does." I had a great match with Dennis, who later became a close friend. So Gustl kept me on in the tournament.

At this time, I got a lot of challenges from wrestlers, like Molnar and a Turk called Mustafa. They were national champions, and they thought they were very good at catch wrestling. And because I was so weakened, they thought this was the time to have a shot at me. But they made a mistake, because catch wrestling is knowledge. If you're strong, that helps you a lot, but the basics are just pure knowledge. Catch wrestling is a combination of knowledge, heart condition, and strength, in that order. That's why catch-as-catch-can is great.

Brunswick Ten-pin Bowling was just then being pushed in Germany. We were doing a promotion at the wrestling tournament, and that's where I met my wife, Ursula. Ulla, we called her. Ulla was doing a world tour with the American female world champion who was promoting Brunswick Bowling. I met her in Nuremberg, where Brunswick Bowling had just started. They came down to the wrestling tournament, and I was in the ring. She was in the front row, and our eyes met; that was the start of the end of my single days. Then we got invited to play ten-pin bowling, and the next day to promote bowling in Germany. She was there, and later on, she began to teach me how to bowl. About 18 months later, she came to England and we got married.

A few years later, before the birth of my son, Spencer, I was reading the Sunday newspaper, and she was making dinner (she was a great cook). On the front page of the newspaper was the headline "The Richest Man in the World, the Nizam of Hyderabad, Is Dead." So I turned the paper to show her. I said, "Look what I gave up for you." There was a picture of the Nizam's granddaughter, the one who had shown considerable interest in me when I was in India. The next thing I knew, I was wearing the dinner she was making. That's how my mother was, too: a wildcat.

The Sambanderak family of Thailand, connected with the royal family there, sent their children to the University of Manchester and Salford while I was in Japan. They stayed at my mother's house. They used to send my mother to Thailand. Once, they gave her a very rare solid gold and jade standing Buddha and a gold chain. She was at a bus stop one night, going home, and some young toughs came up and tried to snatch it off her neck. Well, she beat the living shit out of them with her umbrella and protected it. She'd give nothing up. Like I said earlier, I come from a complete fighting family.

Now, in England at the time, everyone who could look after himself got introduced to the Sabinis and the British mafia. They put a guy named Bill Benny into running all the clubs in the north of England—the sporting men's clubs in Liverpool, Blackburn, Bolton, and all those places around Lancashire. He also had the high society clubs in Manchester. He would bring over people like Frank Sinatra and Judy Garland. The Beatles and all those rock bands started in the workingmen's clubs. The Beatles started at a very minimal wage. Through Benny, I got to meet a lot of people, like the Beatles. When ten-pin bowling came to England and the Beatles were starting to get famous, I was just getting to the British Championship stage and was getting famous, too. Brunswick Bowling set up matches with entertainers; we'd play the wrestlers against the Beatles, or we'd play soccer against the boxers or the jockeys, for charity. I got to meet comedians, like Harry Secombe, and a lot of the British actors, movies stars, and sports people, including the players for Manchester United.

About that time, I headed over to Japan. In Japan, IWE (International Wrestling Enterprise) and the JWA (Japan Pro Wrestling Alliance) were opposition promoters, and the latter had Karl Gotch. I landed in Japan for IWE, as a counter to Gotch.

From Japan, I was going to go back to England, but Dave Ruhl, who was with Stu Hart's promotion, told me to come to Calgary. Ruhl's uncle was Pete Sauer (a.k.a. Ray Steele). In England, I'd heard a lot about how good Ray Steele was. In Calgary, I wrestled Jack Bence. The match was so good that Stu said, "Come back and wrestle at Calgary Stampede." I finished up wrestling Dory Funk Jr. to a one-hour draw. And then Dory Funk said, "Billy, you've got to come to America." That's how I got my first introduction into the Americas. I went back briefly to England, and then to Japan again, followed by Singapore and Hong Kong. There, someone got in touch with me and said, "Come out for Jim Barnett." So I won the World Championship in Australia that Barnett was promoting.

World Champion.

CHAPTER FOUR
THE BUSINESS

Wrestling in those days was very hard. A lot of the matches had no time limits. Back then, there was no "Mixed Martial Arts," only what we used to call private matches. They were private because a lot of it was against the law. For most private matches, only about 20 to 50 people were there, but most bettors made a lot of big money.

If you go back to around 1912, the biggest promoter of sports was the National Sporting Club, which was made up of the English lords. They controlled most sport in those days. For example, they brought Jack Johnson over to fight the British champion. He won. Then they backed him to go to Australia to fight Burns for the World Boxing Championship. They'd pay all the expenses, plus they'd pay for him to go over on the ship, the *Queen Elizabeth*, but he had to promise to do two things: pay them back from the money that he won by winning the World Championship, and defend the title in England one time, which he never did. Because of that, no black man was allowed to fight for a British Championship from 1912 until 1948, when Dick Turpin (Randy Turpin's older brother) became the first black middleweight champion.

The great wrestler from the East in those days was the Great Gama, and Stanislaus Zbyszko was the American heavyweight champion. The British invited both to wrestle at the Harringay Arena, which was the largest arena in Great Britain. Gama beat Zbyszko inside of 12 or 18 seconds or some such ridiculously short time. Ten years earlier, when Zbyszko was in his prime, he had gone through India and wrestled Gama. They'd wrestled an hour draw in the Gusti style. Ten years later, the British wanted to find out who was the best, so they brought Gama from India and Zbyszko from America. Zbyszko was at the end of his career. Ed Lewis was the world champion, but they brought the American champion Zbyszko over instead.

Up until the '40s, guys in pro boxing and real wrestling had to make money any way they could. Wrestlers would try to find promoters who could promote a match to the rugby stadiums or the soccer stadiums. There was no television. Very little was heard on the radio, because the average working-class person couldn't afford a radio. A lot of people couldn't read and write, so posters or newspapers didn't work. People went around with town criers, saying something like, "In two weeks from now, Zbyszko is going to fight the Great Gama" or "Gotch is going to fight Hackenschmidt." That's how it was done in the old days. With television, you've got 15 and 20 matches on the card, lots of lights and glitter, and thousands of people watching; there was none of that in the old days. It was just two fighters, like in the old bare-knuckle days or the early days of pro boxing.

Alf Robinson with his belt, working for a carnival in Ireland, taking all comers.

Being a champion wasn't enough. Fighters had to make money for their families. So they'd fight at state fairs or local fairs. They'd rig up a tent for what they call "carnivals" in America or what we call "fairs" in England. They'd show a bit of a match of guys sparring and challenge anybody in the audience. They'd invite everybody in to see these guys wrestle, but then there was an open challenge for anybody to come in and challenge the wrestler. The audience had to pay to see these challengers take on the touring fighters.

A week's wage in those days was around $12. The challengers might get $24 if they won or if they could last three rounds with any of the fighters. But, of course, none of them won or lasted that long. That's not the point, though. There were all these guys who thought they were tough and came to challenge the carnies. And the carnival wrestlers knew a few submissions, which they learned from guys like John Pesek, Clarence Ecklund, or Ray Steele, and with

My excruciatingly painful set-up for the banana-split pin.

which they could beat anyone if they got challenged. Unfortunately, it's like having dessert without having the salad, soup, and main course.

These carnival guys weren't facing other catch wrestlers. They just needed to beat the local coal miner or tough guy. So although they called themselves great catch wrestlers, they were second-rate guys—with great hearts, no doubt—who knew a few submissions. They never knew how to set up a guy without using brute force. Later on, as the old-timers started retiring, promoters didn't want great wrestlers anymore, since they couldn't control them. By that time, it had become a game of big money. With television, the promoters wanted control of everything.

In the early days, though, when arena matches were offered, most promoters were retired wrestlers. The wrestling business was still very good then. The promoters selected the guys who would wrestle and choose where to promote the match—in New York, Minneapolis, Chicago, Los Angeles, Miami, or wherever. Obviously, wrestling being as tough as it was, the fighters were not going to go through five matches in a short time without somebody getting really badly hurt. So what they used to do is go to the gym and have a private gym match with their two top guys; they would wrestle—"out to shoot," as Americans would say, or "have the pull" as the Wigan guys would say—to find out who was the best. Then they'd go to the next town and do exactly the same thing, except this time they wouldn't be trying to hurt each other. The match would be the same, so they could get paid for five different matches instead of just one; the private gym match was a shoot and the rest were "re-enactments" of that match. Somebody was going to get hurt if they didn't do it that way, because they were very good. But there were those who would try to double-cross you and shoot during one of the "re-enactments." We always needed to watch out. Such matches were called working matches. Nobody watching, not even great wrestlers, knew if it was real or not.

Later on, wrestling matches became a show where audiences wanted to see very young, athletic-looking guys instead of older guys, even though the old-timers were actually far superior in their skills than the younger wrestlers. Young guys sold the television shows a little better, which is what's happening even now in pro wrestling. Guys like Gorgeous George, who was a carnie wrestler, really accelerated the change of pro wrestling into more show than sport. At least now they don't sell it as real wrestling. They sell it as "show wrestling," and, no doubt, it's a great show to watch. Vince Jr. has done more than any other promoter in the history of wrestling worldwide. He's got real wrestlers doing the show wrestling. You've got Olympic wrestlers in there, and MMA fighters who have come from pro wrestling. But the actual show is a show.

Unfortunately, the people outside watching it think

all wrestlers are showmen. That's not true. There's real wrestling out there, and there are still real wrestlers, and the champions are still real champions. Lou Thesz was probably the greatest of all professional world champions, and for one reason: he conducted himself professionally inside the ring, in the gym, outside the ring, in the business world, and with the gentry (royal families) around the world. Everybody respected professional wrestling because of Lou Thesz. He may not have been the best competitive catch wrestler, but he certainly was the best world champion *for the pro wrestling business.*

Lou Thesz and I became good friends. He always tried to tell me that Ed "Strangler" Lewis was the best wrestler in the same way that I felt Billy Joyce was the best. Billy Joyce told me that George Gregory was the best. I guess I've been known as the best, in my time. A lot of the greats have a certain period of time when they're unbeatable, but nothing lasts forever. In most cases back then, with the old-time mats and wrestling on grass, and no sports medicine, injuries were a big reason why the best often lasted a very short period of time.

Lou was older than Karl Gotch, and Gotch was 12 years older than me, so Lou had to be, say, 15 or 16 years older than me. I never actually wrestled him, but he knew Gotch and so knew that I could get the job done. One time Lou refereed a match with Verne Gagne and me when Gagne and I weren't getting on very well. During that match, I was having my way with Gagne. "Look at this, Lou. What do you think of this, Lou?" And Thesz said, "Billy, take it easy. He's the boss." Thesz knew a few of the moves from the time that he had spent with the old-timers before he got into the NWA.

Thesz had a strong bias against Pesek. That came about because Pesek tried to beat Ed Lewis—anytime Ed Lewis was up to match his opponents, it was in the contract that the match was open. If you want to shoot or try to beat me, do it.

Ed Lewis was very sick with boils in those days, and it was a championship match at the Garden. Pesek was a middleweight-cum-light-heavyweight. So what happened was Pesek tried to beat Lewis. It was a hard match, and Lewis won. Lou never forgave Pesek for trying to beat Lewis, and Ed Lewis, I guess, was pissed off about it, too, because Pesek never got promoted around that area again, unless, of course, they had a problem and needed some policing. Lou would never admit that Pesek was a great wrestler, even though he really was. Pesek was probably the best in the world in his weight class in his time. Later on, when Pesek was at the end of his career and wanted to go into the NWA, old as he was then, Lou blackballed Pesek from being able to wrestle in the NWA; Lou had a lot of power in the NWA at that time.

Bert Assirati once challenged Lou Thesz when Thesz wrestled at the Royal Albert Hall in London. Assirati was a street fighter, an exceptionally powerful guy who could wrestle, plus he had the heart of a lion. He was like five-foot-six or five-foot-seven, 280 pounds, and as thick as he was wide. He was a catcher on the high trapeze in the circus when he was 13 years old; that's how strong he was. He could get two 90-pound dumbbells, one in each hand, and hold them out wide in the crucifix position. I've seen him with a 56-pound dumbbell in each hand, swinging them once into a back somersault. He was a sadist and a masochist. He not only liked to hurt people (two of his opponents died in the ring while wrestling him), but he also didn't mind getting hurt.

Assirati had broken away from Joint Promotions and organized an opposition promotion in England. George Gregory and Billy Joyce both challenged him because they were wrestling for Joint Promotions, but he wouldn't have anything to do with either of them. Assirati didn't have the technique needed to be thought of as a good catch wrestler, but he was still very dangerous. However, when Thesz was the world champion and he came to England, Assirati made it known in the newspapers that he was challenging Thesz. So, in response, they had the police waiting for him when he came to the arena. Though they didn't arrest Assirati, they would not allow him into the Royal Albert Hall either.

When I first came to the United States, Lou Thesz had a lot of respect for Karl Gotch, and Karl had a lot of respect for Lou. But then something happened and things changed. They were both extremely stubborn. If their mind was set and you disagreed with them, that was it. Karl and I nearly got into a street fight in Tokyo because I named my son Spencer. He hardly spoke to me for three months. To Karl, I should have called him "Thor" or "Odin" or some other Nordic god's name. I called him Spencer after Winston Churchill, who I thought of very highly, but Gotch couldn't see it. If I had been hard-headed about it, we'd have got into a street fight, or he wouldn't have spoken to me again. That's how a lot of the old-timers were.

Billy Riley was no different. I never heard Billy Riley say anything good about any of the old-time greats; nor did he ever say anything good about me to my face, because, as he explained to me, that would have made me big-headed and I'd stop learning. I never heard him talk about Billy Joyce or Joe Robinson or George Gregory. He never said bad things about them, but he never said they were great, either.

Nobody gave any credit to anybody else. Maybe it was because publicity was mostly word-of-mouth then. So if you said somebody was good, it might get into the minds of the populace that the person you were complimenting was better than you. It is difficult for college wrestlers or Olympic wrestlers nowadays, or even today's MMA guys, to understand something like this, but I can understand because I was among the last really great catch wrestlers.

Back then, you'd have rugby stadiums full just to

watch two guys wrestle on the grass. No mats. No fancy stuff. No time limit. It was a lot harder, especially during spring rains. The second-biggest holiday in England, after Christmas, is Boxing Day, which was the sports day; people would go out and see bare-knuckle fighters or a horse race or a wrestling match or a boxing match. Nowadays, "pro-wrestlers" practise the matches before they go into the ring for a worked match. That would never happen in the old days.

In America, wrestlers used to talk to each other in the ring. English wrestlers from the old catch school didn't need to talk. They knew if somebody got a headlock, and they didn't throw a guy across the ring. If you're going to throw a guy to the ropes, use your shoulder to bump your head out, and throw him in the ropes to do something. It had to be, at the most, three feet away from the ropes; any more than that, and a guy can stop himself. I could tell what my opponent was going to do just by his body position, because I'd learned the basics of catch-as-catch-can. I know what a guy is going to do well before he does it, even in a shoot, because that's what I'm trained to do. I'm trained to know where his weight is, the alignment, so I know where his power is coming from, which direction the power is going to—that's the direction the danger is coming from.

When I turned to pro wrestling, I was shown the pro wrestling game. We never talked there, either. The idea was, who was a good worker? A good worker was someone who could have a match and the people watching, even other wrestlers, would not know that it wasn't real. But that was in Europe. American politics were completely different.

In Europe, you wrestled for any match. You agreed with your promoter in a private meeting what you wanted to be paid for that match. Now, whether the arena was sold out or empty didn't make a difference. Even if the arena was empty, your promoter still paid up. There was no backstabbing like there was in America, especially with the showmen. The showmen in America would slander the old-time wrestlers because they wanted to be in the main event, not the old-timers. They'd say something like, "Oh, he's no good. Don't use him."

Today, for wrestling conditioning, you've got these different machines—you've got all these different calisthenics, like hitting a big tire with these big hammers. That's good if you don't have a sparring partner, but the only way to get into shape for any particular sport is to do it. Billy Riley used to say, "If you want to be a weightlifter, lift weights. If you want to be a runner, go run. But if you want to wrestle, you've got to get on the mat and wrestle and spar. That will give you conditioning faster than any of the other things." With a sparring partner, you're going to get yourself a lot stronger, your technique is going to be advanced, and so is your speed, your knowledge, and your timing. You're going to better understand how to react

Billy just before his famous match against Antonio Inoki.

to whatever an opponent does. Hitting a rubber tire or doing 5,000 squats will not make you a better wrestler.

That's why even big, strong weightlifters and the strongest men in the world, when they get on the mat, are amazed at how strong the wrestlers are. A weight doesn't move; it's just one solid thing that you can control. It's dead weight. Whereas when you're wrestling, you've got a moving weight, and a guy who knows how to use his weight can go from 180 pounds to 500 pounds just by using the angle moving away from you.

For example, look at the sumo wrestlers. All sumo wrestlers, whether the 350- and 400-pounders or the smaller ones, practise splits from when they are three or four years old through to when they retire. They have the big belt, and they grab the belt, try to lean back and lift the opponent's 300 pounds and walk him off the mat. Well, what the opponent does then is arch the legs out backwards and open into the splits position. Now, instead of having 300 pounds close to their body, it's like trying to hold 300 pounds out at arm's length. It just can't be done.

In the old Wigan gym, the coach would get five or six good guys, and you'd go on the mat for an hour and a half or two and a half hours, non-stop. He would send a new guy in every three to five minutes. If you were getting the better of a guy too easy, he'd send somebody else in. *Then* you learn how to make your opponent do all the work, and you don't get tired. That's why some of these old matches were so long, like the Olympic match that lasted 11 hours 40 minutes. That's when they started to cut the time down, because you can't have 700 matches at 11 hours apiece.

When I first came in and started to get mixed up with the MMA and stuff, I said, "Get out of that guard position. You've got to learn to stand up and get away." Ten years later, they've started to realize that what I was telling them was correct. Now, they can't hold guys on the mat, but I was telling them that from my experience years ago.

In a street fight or in a catch match, you don't want to be underneath. If you're underneath with a guy who knows what he's doing, and you can't escape, you're in trouble because you run out of gas. You're using twice or three times the amount of energy by being underneath—carrying his weight and defending yourself. He's using that against you.

With any kind of fight—and both my dad and Billy Riley told me this—you're never fast enough, and you're never good enough. No matter how good or fast you are or how easily you beat a guy, you very well might have *a lot* of trouble with the next guy because of the difference of styles, even though the next guy may not be as good as the first guy. When two of the greatest fighters in the world fight each other, the match can turn miserable and boring because of the clash of styles.

Most fighters or boxers now don't even know how to throw a power punch. When the older fighters threw a punch, it had the full body behind it. They'd rotate the hip and shoulder so the actual punch only travelled six inches but had all the body behind it. Nowadays, the hip goes backwards when the arm goes forward, so there's no power.

I've written this book and made videos so those who are interested can learn these things. The only reason anyone knows about Billy Riley and Pop Charnock is because of Karl Gotch and me. Nobody else was talking about them. It's like Waino Ketonen: he beat everybody, and there were plenty more like him—for example, the winners of the German tournaments in the late 1800s and early 1900s.

Ketonen came from Finland, and the Finns had some great wrestlers in the old days. Technique-wise, they were very good. But Ketonen was one of those guys who comes around only once in a hundred years. When he was champion, and even before that, he went all over the world and beat everybody. I think he was only about 155 or 165 pounds. All top wrestlers were tall and lanky. These huge guys with muscles you see in drawings, they are not wrestlers, and that is not a wrestling body; a wrestling body is supple. You've got to be loose. If you saw Billy Joyce, you wouldn't be impressed by his looks, but if you saw him wrestling, you'd realize what an amazing wrestler he was. Power is a combination of strength and speed. Add technique, and you become good.

For example, if you get into a front headlock and you've got to do the switch behind, there's a technique that makes it easy. All amateurs make the switch, but they do it with power alone. There's a technique, and there's a great counter to it as well. It's not easy, though. When I was first shown the move, for some reason, I just couldn't get it.

For one month, I went to the gym three or four times a week, for two to three hours at a time; all I did on the mat was try to do the switch. "Do it again." "Do it again." These words rang inside my head, giving me nightmares. After one month, Billy Riley said to me, "Forget it. You're never going to get it. I don't want to see you try it again."

Well, the next week, the same guy comes in and goes up to the gym to work out. Billy Riley calls me to come up to spar. First thing, I grab his head and arm;

he kneels down in a position to do the switch. I do the counter so perfectly that the guy is flat down, and I've got a top wristlock submission. It was all over in about 15 seconds, and Billy was smiling.

Afterwards, Billy Riley, Joe Robinson, and I went back to Billy's house. The three of us are having tea, and Billy's telling me how I could have got it better! He never said I did anything well. Billy Riley was that way even with the best, like Bob Robinson, a.k.a. Billy Joyce. Riley said, "For 12 years, Bob was the dumbest guy we ever had in the gym." Both Joe (Bob's brother) and Billy spent more time with him than anybody: when Bob finished his shift at the coal mine, either Joe or Billy would be waiting for him.

Bob would go straight to the gym, work out there, and then he'd go home. But when he got home, Joe would be there and would go over it all again with him. This went on for 12 years, and he just didn't get it. Then, overnight, something just clicked. It was like somebody opened his mind to learning how to learn. Then, all that training over the years, it just mushroomed out. He was unbelievable, technique-wise. If you were to ask Karl Gotch, he'd tell you. Billy Joyce played with Gotch. Billy Joyce played with me, until the age difference caught up with him. As he got older and started to go down, I was coming up and learning, reaching my prime.

It's all about being loose and open to learning. Today, nobody knows how to ride. It's not just the jiu-jitsu guys; even amateur wrestlers have no idea of how to get pressure and control. You go back in my time, or well before, and you had guys that were pure leg-wrestlers. Guys like Joe Robinson, who was so loose or supple he could put a dime on his toe and pick it up with his teeth.

Today, promoters use football and basketball players to draw crowds. Football players aren't wrestlers. As my dad or Billy Riley would say, they couldn't even fight their way out of a bloody paper bag. Their immense strength and their popularity as football players brings them into pro wrestling. Think about all the big-mouthed, showy football and basketball players nowadays; how many of them have you seen do any good in MMA? No football player has beaten any of the decent MMA guys, no matter how big and strong he is, or how good a shape he thinks he's in. It's a completely different game.

In earlier days, if promoters and TV management liked a certain guy—"Oh, he's a good-looking guy; I'd like to watch him fight"—they'd push that guy to get him in the forefront, giving him matches with guys he could beat. Later, they changed the game so all the guys would be "show" guys that anyone could beat. There's immense money involved today.

With the old-timers, this didn't work, because the "show" guys couldn't beat them. For instance, Dick Hutton was a great amateur wrestler, the smoothest of all the American heavyweight wrestlers during his time. When I say he was smooth, I mean technique-wise. He was as much power as knowledge. His style was like catch-as-catch-can. He became a very good professional wrestler. He didn't have the "show" or the "drawing power," but he had the ability to beat *everybody*.

Though football players had immense drawing power for pro wrestling promoters, they always had a real wrestler around them. Verne Gagne would use Karl Gotch, me, Khosrow Vaziri, Brad Rheingans, and other guys as policemen. It was really TV that changed everything. Real catch wrestling champions weren't good-looking, athletic young guys with fantastic bodies. They were knowledgeable men that have been through the mill, and to become a champion any-where, you had to be the best.

THE GUYS

In my day, probably one of the most dangerous guys was Danny Hodge. Danny was a great amateur wres-tler; he had great hand strength. He boxed profession-ally, too. He was a Golden Gloves champion, and he had the heart of an elephant. He wouldn't say no or quit for anybody, anytime. Danny has to be, without doubt, one of the American greats of all times. I don't know how he'd have done against the old-timers. Once I asked Riley who the best was. He said, "Any

Hall of Fame, 2003, with Danny Hodge.

dog on a given day can win a fight. But if you really want to get to the heart of the whole matter, you'd have to have them fight or wrestle 10 times and see who wins the most matches of the 10." I never got to spar with Lou, but with Gotch, I did. I could take him down and get behind him, and control the thing the whole time. However, the 12 years difference in age between us made a big difference. Gotch was getting close to 50, I think he was 48 when I did that, so I'd be 34 or 35. I could have made him tap-out in my prime, but I had too much respect for him. I beat Billy Joyce, but it's the same thing—age difference. I don't know how it would have been if Gotch or Joyce were at their best and I was at my best.

In Japan, when I was coaching UWFI, the two top young guys were Sakuraba and Tamura. Although Tamura beat Sakuraba the last two times they fought,

UWFi Wrestling.

I would say that Sakuraba at his best would beat Tamura at his best seven or eight out of ten. Tamura is exceptionally dangerous because he is unpredictable. Sometimes, out of nowhere, he does really goofy, out of this world stuff—even he doesn't know that he's going to do. Just like a street fighter, he can always catch his opponent unawares. But, based on one match, you cannot say about anyone, "Okay. He beat him. He can beat him anytime." It doesn't work that way.

The business side of pro wrestling was different; that's why what we call a policeman comes into it.

Like Ray Steele protected Thesz. You'd have to go through Ray Steele to get to Thesz, and Thesz would watch the match to see the challenger's ability (there were no videos or TV, so this was a way to watch the challenger). I've done it in many countries for different promoters, and four or five times for Gagne, against guys who have challenged.

Winning IWA World, 1969.

We had a guy that came into Milwaukee in the early '70s. I forget his name. He was trying out all different sports—pro football, basketball, and boxing, and then he wanted to try wrestling. So Gagne asked me to take care of it, and I agreed. We discussed it with the promoter there, Dennis Hilgart, because they were taping it. Gagne said to me, "Billy, let it go 10 minutes. Don't just go in and beat him." I said, "You've got to be joking. I could get poked in the eye, or kicked in the balls." You never know what may happen. He said, "No, no, Billy. We need it for publicity." Had I known better, I would never have done that, especially for a guy like Gagne, who later double-crossed me in many ways, money-wise. But I didn't know better.

I went in and I played with the guy for 10 minutes. Back then, the timekeeper used to tell the referee the time, so I told the ref, "Tell me when it's nine minutes." So in nine minutes, he said, "Nine minutes, Billy." I said, "Okay." Bang. I took the guy down, cranked his neck a little bit, and he was already screaming. So I finished him off with a top wristlock, and instead of grabbing the hands, I got the wrist bone over and pulled it in, basically cranking his head and the arm at the same time. As I do so, he's crying, and he's tapping me with his free hand, and he's saying, "Yeah, yeah, yeah!"

I said, "Ref, can you hear that?"

"I don't hear it, Billy. Did you say something?"

The guy is screaming. I could hear his elbow going. Just before it's going to break I told the referee to say "okay." The guy got on live television later and said, "Listen. I've tried pro football; I've tried pro boxing. There is no doubt whatsoever that pro wrestling is the nastiest, hardest, most dangerous sport there is." What he didn't realize was that he was with a guy who knew what he was doing.

Recently, I was watching a television talk show and the host was interviewing the famous pro wrestler "the Rock." He talked about a street fight that his grandfather, Peter Maivia, who was also a pro wrestler, got into. Well, he didn't mention that I was the one that his grandfather got into the street fight with; besides, he got the facts wrong. As the Rock correctly said, Peter Maivia would want to fight anybody whenever he'd had a couple of drinks. When this incident happened, we were in Japan doing wrestling shows.

After the matches, we went to a restaurant to eat. Peter Maivia, John da Silva, George Gordienko, Frank Valois—national champion, Olympic wrestler, and a very good catch wrestler—and a few other guys were there. In Japan in those days, they had this set menu that you had to order from in a certain way. For example, if the menu had fish and chips or roast beef and mashed potatoes with peas, there was no way you could get the french fries with the roast beef, or the mashed potatoes with the fish. Something upset George about this menu, and he went off. Peter joins in with George. So it's an hour and a half, with 10 of us there plus the interpreter, waiting just to get our orders in, and Peter keeps messing it up. So I say, "Peter, keep your big mouth shut. Let everybody order. Let's get our food and then go our separate ways," which finally we did.

Peter and George leave and go one way. John da Silva and I go the other. We end up close to the hotel, and George and Peter see me and John walking up. John must have known something was going on. He said, "Oh, shit. I don't have anything to do with this." John leaves me and goes into the hotel. I walk up and say, "Peter, George, what's happening?" Peter starts screaming and shouting at me and pushing me. I say, "Peter, you're drunk. You messed everybody up." But he wants to fight.

He throws a couple of punches, which I block easily; I grab him and hold him around the waist. I say, "Peter, stop it. I mean, I really don't want to hurt you." He then tries to bite me on the neck. Luckily, I pull my jaw down because I've been trained. However, he bites me straight through my cheek—I have four or five holes in my face where his teeth went through. Blood is spurting out.

When I see the blood, I flat out end the fight right then and there. It lasts all of 15 seconds. Peter is knocked out and stays out for 20-odd minutes. Gordienko pulls me off because he thinks I am going to do more damage. Peter has his nose broken and two black eyes, but I have to go to the hospital to get my face stitched up and get injections for the human bite. When I'm going back to the hotel, some guys warn me, "Oh, don't go back. Peter's going to kill you. We've got a new hotel for you." I say, "Fuck you." I make them take me back to the hotel.

The next morning, I beat on his door. He opens it. I push him into his room and lock the door. I said, "You tried to kill me. You tried to bite me in the neck. You bit through my face. You're lucky you're not in the bloody hospital or dead. But if you want to try now . . ." But he's sobered up enough to know he has no chance. Then I walk over to Gordienko's room and do the same thing with Gordienko. It later came out when I was talking to Peter that George had instigated the whole thing.

The Rock said his grandfather bit my eye out. The only eye operations that I've ever had were when I got hit in the eye as a young kid and switched from boxing to wrestling. It's likely that Peter's wife, the Rock's grandmother, spread that story. The Maivias later became promoters in Hawaii. In fact, Peter invited me to Hawaii to wrestle for him, which I did. We became friends afterwards. It was just that Peter, like the Rock said, used to go bonkers.

It is common to hear guys say, "This guy beat that guy." But they would have never seen the fight in the first place, and they don't know anything about real street fighting or real catch wrestling. Sometimes, you may have just showed someone a couple of things, and all of a sudden they "trained with Karl Gotch" or "trained with Billy Robinson." That happened all the time. For example, a close friend of mine, Johnny Eagles, came over to the States. Cowboy Bill Watts, a booker for Leroy McGuirk, called me in Minnesota and asked me how good Johnny Eagles was, since he'd gone to Wigan and wrestled with me. I burst out laughing. I said, "He came to my gym and had two workouts with me, because he wanted to borrow money from me to buy a car." He paid me back the money later, but he never came back to the gym. He never catch wrestled in his life, but he was a great worker.

Once, I told Karl Gotch that I was going to go in for Verne. He said, "That bald-headed, spindly legged old bastard can't wrestle his way out of a paper bag. He's just a bully. If he knows that he can beat you, he'll beat the living shit out of you." But all bullies are that way. Gagne has a great heart to win, but when he knows he's with somebody better, he will make an excuse to make sure he doesn't get beat.

Gagne had a shoot with Ruffy Silverstein and couldn't beat him. Afterwards, he said, "Oh, the only reason I didn't beat Silverstein is I hurt my ankle and broke three of my fingers." They were supposed to do a draw, and Gagne didn't want to do a draw. Silverstein didn't want to do a job or lose. So Verne said, "Fuck it, try." He couldn't beat Silverstein. Now, Silverstein was in a bad situation. He was getting older, and Gagne was a promoter of the sport, so if he upset Gagne, he'd have been blackballed. So he said, "Okay, I'll do what I said. I'll do a draw, but there's no way you're going to beat me."

As much as Gagne tried, he couldn't get the job done. I know Lou did shoot with Silverstein and won, but then, Lou was *a lot* bigger than Silverstein. I asked Lou about that, and he said to me, "Billy, Silverstein was very capable and very dangerous for 20 or 25 minutes. But over the long haul, he faded away."

My journey in the USA started in Hawaii. There, I

went to visit Lord James Blears—a very good friend of my uncle and father, having gone to the same school. Blears was a very good swimmer—senior Hawaiian champion—and loved Hawaii. One of his sons became a world champion surfer. He was highly decorated.

Because he was too young to enter the Second World War in the British navy or army, he joined the Dutch navy as a radio operator. He was torpedoed three times and taken prisoner aboard a Japanese submarine. The prisoners were all tied together, and the Japanese were chopping their heads off. Blears managed to escape and even saved the lives of a lot of the other prisoners. He got medals from the king of England, the Dutch queen, and the Americans. At the war trials for the Japanese, he was called in to give testimony about the submarine incident.

Lord Blears was in with the local wrestling promotion. At that time, he was a co-promoter with a guy named Ed Francis. He got me to stay in Hawaii for about 18 months. There, I met Verne Gagne when he came over with his family on vacation. We were tag team partners in one of the matches, and then he watched me wrestle single matches. Verne gave me the opportunity to live in America. He asked me to train his son. I landed on the U.S. mainland in 1972. Later, Verne had a camp with people like Ric Flair, Jim Brunzell, the Iron Sheik, Sgt. Slaughter, and Ken Patera.

The Iron Sheik (Khosrow Vaziri) was a six- or

seven-time national champion on the greatest amateur team in the world in those days. He managed to escape from Iran at a time when Takhti and other wrestlers on the Iranian Olympic wrestling team, who were also bodyguards of the Shah, were murdered. Takhti was probably one of the greatest light heavyweight Olympians and freestyle wrestlers of all time. Ayatollah Khomeini was coming back from Paris; the revolution was about to start in Iran, and a lot of the wrestlers were going to back Ayotallah Khomeini, so the Shah gave the order. Fortunately, Khosrow Vaziri wasn't there at that particular time. He was brought in to coach the Greco-Roman team that was starting at the University of Minnesota, which still has a great Greco team. They wanted to be able to pay Khosrow a bit extra, so they got him into pro wrestling; that's how he came to the camp.

The Iron Sheik was a very good amateur, but with a big head and a big mouth. Amateur doesn't match well against catch-as-catch-can. He thought he could beat me, so he said, "Get behind me. You can't turn me over or beat me." He went down in the defence position. He didn't know about catch-as-catch-can, ankle submissions, neck cranks, and double wristlocks, so I just knelt on his thigh in the way that we do in Wigan. He couldn't walk for nearly two days and couldn't work out or come to the camp for two weeks. The coach from the University of Minnesota called Gagne

Hall of Fame 2003, with Destroyer.

and said, "Listen. We want Khosrow to learn how to wrestle, not get hurt."

In Minneapolis one day, they told me to be at the TV station at two o'clock. When I got there, they had done a lot of taping. Of course, I'd been to Europe and Asia, where we didn't have television. Even when they televised wrestling matches, they didn't do interviews like the Americans do, so I didn't know anything about that yet. So I was in the ring, and I think it was with a Japanese wrestler called Kobayashi, and it was my first match on television. I beat him, but what ruined the match was somebody saying, "Oh, Nick Bockwinkel can beat you." The guy was really obnoxious. He was really screaming into the ring—you know, an excited fan. So I jumped over the top rope and paint-brushed him—picked him up and slapped him to and fro, and then I set him down. He was quiet for the rest of the day.

When I got into the dressing room after the match, Gagne was with Wally Carbo, the promoter, and they were going crazy. "You can't do that in America. Anybody can sue anybody else in America, and we could lose our licence!"

As it happened, they gave the guy a few free tickets to the matches that were coming up, and everything was fine. I didn't know that the station could have been sued; I had never heard of anybody suing another person in England.

Anyway, we had fun in those days. I don't know how we all got together, but Nick Bockwinkel, Harley Race, Dory Funk Jr. (from the NWA), and I (from the AWA) were all on the same tour. The ski season was coming up, so we decided to go out and ski together. Of course, each of us thought we were better than the other at skiing. You should have seen us! Everything was a contest. Especially when you got Harley Race and Dory Jr. together. Nick and I were doing all the nice, beautiful turns, but with Harley and Dory, it was like the Indy 500. Because they went so crazy and challenged us, you got four professional wrestling world champions going down a hill like runaway express trains—crossing each other's paths, knocking into

The champion in Florida.

each other, and taking bigger bumps and falls than they had ever done in the ring. Afterwards, we said, "What were we doing?" But that competition was always there between us.

Those were great guys—Dory and Harley and Nick. In pro wrestling, unlike in football teams, the guys usually do not go out together; you very rarely socialize with people that you're going up against, unless it's for charity or a dinner and you've both been invited to. Then it's cordial, but there's no friendship lost between any of the top competitors.

So these guys were special, but not everyone was like that. It reminds me of an incident in Calgary, when I wrestled Jack Bence. I got into Calgary a few weeks before the Stampede. I went to the dressing room one day, and there are four big guys in the dressing room. Now, of course, this being my first time in North America, I didn't know any American or Canadian wrestlers other than those I'd met in my travels around the world. Well, they were huge guys, so I thought, they've got to be wrestlers.

They were talking while I was getting dressed and just starting to warm up, and I realized that the conversation was not like a wrestler's conversation. It was more about football. They were football players from the Calgary Stampeders. I asked, "Excuse me. Are you guys wrestlers?" They said, "No, we're football players." I said, "This is the wrestling dressing room. Could you step outside?" One of them replied, "No, we want to stay in here. We want to see Stu Hart." "You can wait for him outside," I said. "This is the wrestling dressing room." The same one replied, "Well, who do you think is going to put us out?" I explained to them very nicely that I'd like them to get out while I'm getting dressed because I didn't know them. I mean, they may steal from me or my clothes or whatever. There were few words said, but they left shortly afterward. One of them, Wayne Coleman (better known later as Superstar Billy Graham), left with a little more than his feelings hurt.

By the time Coleman became a pro wrestler, I had already moved to Minnesota. Gagne and Carbo wanted him to come up from California, but Coleman insisted that I had to sign a contract with Verne saying we wouldn't have any matches against each other, and if a match did come up where we were both in the ring, like a battle royale or a tag team match, then I wouldn't hurt him. Superstar Billy Graham had to have that on paper before he'd come up to Minnesota.

I worked with the AWA (American Wrestling Association) for a number of years. I was world tag team champion, once with Gagne and once with "the Crusher." Then I was AWA champion for 24 hours, until they changed the decision on me. In 1974, Gagne produced the movie *The Wrestler*. It featured Ed Asner, Verne, Dusty Rhodes, Dick Murdoch, Harold Sakata (Oddjob from *Goldfinger*), and me.

Harold Sakata (a.k.a. Tosh Togo) and I were close friends even before I came to the States. When they were casting *Goldfinger*, an Indian-English actor named Milton Reid, who made a lot of movies in those days, was in the running for the character Oddjob. When the producers brought Sakata in, Milton Reid—who was a lot bigger than Harold—told him that if he ever wrestled anywhere in England, Reid would challenge him. So the promoters put me on every card that Harold did, and I travelled around with him so that if this guy challenged, they'd say, "Well, okay, you have to wrestle and beat Billy Robinson first," and I'd take care of the situation. That's how Harold and I became friends.

I used to do the same with Primo Carnera when we were both in Spain. I used to go around with him as a policeman, in case somebody played smart. He was older then and was just doing exhibition matches anyway. But you always get somebody that thinks they're tough, and they're going to take a shot at a guy that was the world boxing champion. Of course, he was a wrestler first before becoming a boxer.

Jack Brisco was another champion that I met. The first time I was in a match with Jack, we were in Brisbane, Australia. I had just won the World Championship. During the match, Jack was trying to show how good he was, so I kind of showed him a Wigan

Billy Robinson applying the Boston Crab.

hold in the ring, and he ended up in the hospital. He was a very good amateur champion and a super nice guy. He became the NWA champion after Dory Funk.

In Australia, we stayed at Southern Star, a big hotel in Melbourne. It was a big name then; it was one of those very posh old English-type hotels. Anyway, it's late at night, and Jack Brisco calls me over to his room. I come to the room, and we start talking about American and English amateur wrestling and catch wrestling, and then the old American shooters and

British shooters. I don't know what a "shooter" is; they are just catch wrestlers to me. Anyway, once I figure out that a shooter was just an American word for a catch wrestler, we get into it. He has been introduced to a couple of wristlocks, but he doesn't know how to do a double wristlock. So I show him a few, and the cross-faces. I show him how to really crank it up, and the different angle submissions. And we're laughing and joking.

Now, I should have known better because, just a week earlier, Brisco and Dick Murdoch had pulled a nasty practical joke on me. They had introduced me to American football. A game between Texas and Oklahoma was being shown in Australia on television. We were watching it live. Dick Murdoch was from Texas, and Jack was from Oklahoma. They were chewing tobacco and drinking bourbon and Coke. I had never done any of this. They had me drinking bourbon and Coke, which I hated, and Jack introduced me to chewing tobacco. As I was chewing it, I asked "What do you do?" They said, "Oh, just swallow the juice, and spit the tobacco out." So I believed them and drank the juice; I not only spit the tobacco out, but I also puked all over the place. They pulled this rib on me a week before, so I should have known better.

It's maybe four or five o'clock in the morning, and Jack and I have been talking wrestling all the while. So, I've stripped off and am in my underpants, showing him different holds. We hear a noise outside, so Jack says, "Oh, that's the paper, Billy. Go get the paper for me." So I walk out into the hallway in my underpants to pick up the paper, and he locks the door. I'm in the best hotel in the whole of Australia, full of rich and educated people, trying to call down to get the key to my room. I go upstairs. I manage to get upstairs by taking the safety stairs, and not the elevator, because there were people going in and out. I'm trying to hide from everybody. Well, somebody did see me sneaking around in my underpants, and they sent security up. I tell them my story; they laugh and open the door for me and leave.

Another funny incident happened when I was in Calgary wrestling Dory Funk. We got invited to an evening with the premier of Alberta at his house. He wanted to take us to Banff, a big banquet with tuxedos and bow ties and the whole deal. So the premier's wife said, "So now, don't forget, Billy, tomorrow."

I reply, "Yes, I'll come and knock you up about eight o'clock." Now, in England, that's a common expression for "I'll see you at eight o'clock." There we had professional "knocker-uppers," people that used to come to the tiered houses and knock on the bedroom window or beat on the door to get people up in time for their shift. Of course, I didn't know what that meant in America or Canada until they explained it to me. I was extremely embarrassed.

Gordienko was really the best in America in those days. Of all the guys I've wrestled around the world, he was probably the naturally strongest that I've ever met. He was very strong in a number of ways. I don't know anything about poundages and stuff, but by wrestling strength, he was the strongest man I've ever met on the mat. The Hungarian Josef Kovacs came next. He was second in the World Amateur Championships when he was like 17 or 18. He was naturally strong, just unbelievably powerful.

Gordienko was to become the NWA heavyweight champion, but then he got blacklisted and had to leave the U.S. Joe Pazandak, a very good old-time catch wrestler, had trained him and brought him into pro wrestling. Gordienko was married to Pazandak's daughter. She was the head of the Communist Party in that area of America, and George Gordienko married her during the McCarthy era, when a lot of sportsmen, showmen, and movie stars—like Larry Parks and Paul Robeson—had their careers ended.

To train for the 1948 Olympics, Gagne wanted sparring partners, and George wasn't a pro wrestler at this time. He was just working out with Pazandak. Verne didn't like Pazandak because he was a lot older, and a much better catch wrestler. Verne knew it, and he didn't want anything to do with Pazandak. So he brought George over; George was young in those days. Verne said, "Okay, go down. I'll get behind you. Try to escape." And Gordienko went *bam!* He exploded and escaped. So then Gagne got down for Gordienko, and said, "Okay. Now I'll escape. You try to hold me down," and Gordienko held him down until Verne quit. He just held him down. Verne no longer wanted to spar with him.

When Gordienko's wife got in trouble for being with the Communist Party, Gordienko was kicked out of America. He went back to Manitoba, and from there he went to England and taught at an art school. He was a great artist.

Gordienko knew quite a bit of the old catch-as-catch-can, so they wanted to see if he would stand a chance against Bert Assirati. The promoters were going to pay, so they brought Billy Joyce down from Wigan to London and got Gordienko, who was living in London, to the gym. Gordienko was supposed to work out with Billy Joyce (they were paying Billy to spar with him), but he didn't want to. Billy said to him straight, "Look. We're not going to hurt each other. They just want to see how capable you are. Just go in and feel me out and let me feel you out."

I don't know if George didn't trust him or if he thought Billy Joyce would beat him, but George got very nervous. Billy would have done just enough to prevent George beating him and to show he was in control, because Billy was that type of guy. George was so nervous that while he was having his rice pudding, he got hold of some ketchup and put it on the pudding. That's a true story. I was there. He just didn't want to have anything to do with Billy Joyce. It was good business for him not to take the chance of getting beaten. Real catch-as-catch-can wrestlers, the real pro wrestlers, weren't scared of anybody or anything. Joe Pazandak, Ed Lewis, Stanislaus Zbyszko were very good. His brother Wladek was technically better than Stanislaus, but I've heard that he didn't have the heart.

Another name that is worth mentioning is Bob Meyers. According to Billy Riley, Meyers was even better than Benny Sherman. Billy should know, because he wrestled them both and worked out with them both. Benny Sherman was the heaviest and Billy was the smallest of the three. Meyers took up the middle. They met up and did what the old carnies did—they went to South Africa, to the gold mines and the diamond mines, challenging everybody.

Even Frank Gotch did this. He would send one of his guys to the lumberjack areas of Minnesota and Canada to get into a camp. Once the guy got in, he would start to work out, wrestling. Then the lumber-jacks would get interested, because everybody was bored. There's nothing to do up there; we're talking late 1890s, early 1900s. Eventually, the guy would say, "I need to get ready to wrestle Frank Gotch for the championship. I need somebody to spar with."

He'd get the youngest and the strongest, the best there, and then he'd work with them every day. After they'd finished their chopping and eating, they'd get out and spar. Everybody'd be watching them, and during this period of time, some of the guys would be getting better and better and better, to where it was taking Gotch's guy an hour to beat them, or maybe he wouldn't beat them at all. Then, two or three days before Gotch was going to come up for the match, the guy would start sparring with them and he'd pretend to hurt his leg, so now he couldn't wrestle. He'd let everybody in the camp know that this kid hurt him.

So while a few would be for cancelling the fight, everyone else would be saying, "Oh no, this is one of us. He can beat Gotch because he's beat this guy." There would be a lot of money bet on the match. Well, Gotch was so far superior that he'd arrive and just play with the guy without anybody knowing that he was really in total control. Gotch would let it go long enough; then he'd just beat the guy, and they'd pick up thousands of dollars, and in those days, that was a tremendous amount of money. That's how they would make money. This was before the promoters got involved. Back then, there were no regular weekly matches, where you go to the arena. The money was not generated selling tickets to an event. It was made on bets. When you had those types of matches, you burned your body out so much with the training plus the actual match that guys got hurt all the time. You couldn't wrestle three or four times a week in those kind of matches.

Also, remember, there were no airplanes in those days. To go to India, you'd get the Great Eastern train from London through Europe, all the way through Turkey into Arabia. It would take months to get around the world. Guys like Waino Ketonen, Billy Riley, and Tom Connors brought catch wrestling to America and the world. Japanese jiu-jitsu guys did the same. They couldn't make any money in Japan, because it wasn't done that way there. So they went around the world, challenging people. That's when they got beat by catch-as-catch-can wrestlers. That's where they picked up the double wristlock and the figure fours (which they call a triangle now), because those were very common holds in catch wrestling.

CHAPTER FIVE

REBIRTH IN JAPAN

Pro wrestling in Japan started with Al Baffert beating Rikidōzan. Baffert was a very good American catch wrestler. He, along with wrestlers from various units in the U.S. Army, put on a show for the American soldiers in Japan. Sumo wrestlers wanted to watch the show, so the Americans got invited to meet with the sumo association and sumo champions. They met at a big, beautiful Japanese-style hotel, with tatami mats. They sat on the floor talking, and finally, they said, "This boy wants to challenge you." That boy happened to be Rikidōzan, who was a young sumo champion at that time. When the young Rikidōzan was asked, "Which wrestler do you want?" He pointed directly at Tosh Togo.

The Great Kusatsu, Billy Robinson, "Thunder" Sugiyama, and George Gordienko in Japan in the late '60s.

Taking nothing away from him, Tosh Togo (a.k.a. Harold Sakata) wasn't a good real wrestler; he was more of a professional wrestler, a showman. He was a very powerful weightlifter, winning a silver medal for weightlifting in the Olympics. He was also scared to death of sumo wrestlers. So Al Baffert took up the challenge from Rikidōzan.

Al told me the story years later when I met him in Japan, where he was refereeing matches. He said, "Rikidōzan was pretty good for about a minute and a half, and then he just faded away." This made sense to me, since the matches in sumo wrestling only last for a short time. There's one big explosion for about 15, 20, or max 30 seconds; if it goes into a minute or a minute and a half or two minutes, the referee stops to let them get their wind back, and starts them again from the same position they were in when the match was stopped.

Before a Japanese tournament; Billy Robinson, George Gordienko, Michael Nador, Ray Hunter, and Peter Maivia (with flag).

They didn't know any submissions, either. They were just very well balanced on their feet. Baffert took Rikidōzan down, got him in a control position, and beat him. Of course, the Japanese version of the story is different, where it was Harold Sakata who fought Rikidōzan, but that's not true. Al Baffert even wrote a book about it, but they wouldn't publish it in Japan because that's not the story they wanted to believe.

Travelling in Japan.

(Rikidōzan was a god over there, like Antonio Inoki. Karl Gotch, too, became the "God of Wrestling" because he taught Inoki. In Japan, everything's got to have a god and everything's got to have a name.)

I had a great time in Japan and made a lot of close friends there. Japan is a great country. I got there through the Japanese Olympic Committee. Rikidōzan had died, and in the Japanese Wrestling Association, the top men were Toyonobori and Giant Baba. Antonio Inoki was young and coming up back then. They had Karl Gotch as a trainer, and there was no one that could handle Karl.

Toyonobori and Giant Baba split after a clash over money: Toyonobori, along with Yoshihara, formed the IWE (International Wrestling Enterprise), while Giant Baba got the big push by the JWA (Japan Pro Wrestling Alliance). Karl was beating everybody and training young Japanese guys in those days. The IWE wanted *somebody* to counteract him, so they got hold of the

Olympic Gold medallist and world champion, Shozo Sasahara. Sasahara called George de Relwyskow (the son of the gold medallist of the same name for England in the 1908 Olympics), who then called Billy Riley to find out who was the best guy in Wigan, and Billy Riley said, "Billy Robinson." That's how I landed in Japan. The Toyonobori organization brought me over to counteract Karl, not realizing that Karl was like my uncle, and that, in fact, my uncle had started Karl in catch-as-catch-can, and that Karl had learned his wrestling in the same gym with the same coaches.

Doing a television interview after winning a match.

Because Karl and I were in opposition to each other in Japan, there was no way we could openly meet or socialize. But we used to find ways to meet somewhere by accident. We'd take our wives with us, we'd have dinner, and also we'd find ways to have private workouts. We'd go to the gym when there was nobody there and spar with each other. That I found very funny.

While in Japan, I ended up winning the tournament, and then, I won the World Championship. After that, the Toyonobi organization asked me to move long-term to Japan with my family.

I was with Karl one day, and I was a bit grumpy. "What's eating you?" he asked.

I said, "I'm having a bit of a problem with the Japanese guys."

He said, "Why?"

Billy upon returning to Japan, this time as a coach. Here Billy is helping the Great Inoue with bridging.

I said, "Well, they're not learning like I'd like them to. It's like they're distracted."

Karl asked me if I had hurt anybody yet.

I said, "No, I'm coaching. I'm not going to hurt them."

Karl said this to me: "This is Japan. This is not England or Europe or America. This is Japan." He said, "Listen to me. Hurt one of them."

I said, "Karl, I don't want to. I can't do that."

Well, whether I wanted it or not, it happened the following week. There was a snowstorm in Tokyo. When Tokyo got snow, their traffic system would grind to a halt. They didn't have it set up like in America, where everything gets cleared away. As I was leaving for the gym, I had a row with my wife, so I was not in a good mood to start with. The student who was going to pick me up was 30 minutes late because of the snow. I was standing out in the snow, and I looked like a bloody snowman by the time he got there, as there was no shelter where I said I'd meet him, and we had no cell phones in those days.

When I got to the gym, I was in a real bad mood. One of the top Japanese boys mouthed off about something. "That's it," I said. I lined them all up, and I wrestled them all, and every time I came to him, I turned on the gas a little bit. Finally, he went mad and actually tried to hurt me. So I broke his arm. As soon as I hurt him, it was like Karl said: a change came over the Japanese boys. The whole situation changed. They took me to the shower, washed my clothes, took me out to eat. As bizarre as it was to me, in Japan, if you're the boss, nobody questions you. In a violence sport or martial arts sport, you've got to prove you're the master. It's not a "he said" deal. Karl knew that, and he tried to tell me, but I didn't believe it until this incident happened. After I established I was the boss, coaching the Japanese was very good.

Billy, while working for All Japan, wrestling Jumbo Tsuruta (and beating him) for the championship.

It's a very different culture; when they need something from you, you're god. They'd do anything for you. But when they've got what they need, then *they* are the boss; they order you around like dogs. Karl

Billy starting a double arm suplex on Inoki as John "Red Shoes" Dugan officiates.

couldn't stand it. Toward the end of my stay in Japan, I couldn't stand it, either. They'd say, "I'm finished with you. Now you can go." You don't do that, not to a European or an American.

The Japanese really helped me when I was at the end of my wrestling career; I had gone through a divorce and got on a bit of a drinking spree. When I was in Minnesota, Inoki called me up and said, "Billy, will you come to Japan?" I was thrilled. Things had gotten so low by that point that I was a manager of a store at a gas station. That was the most boring, miserable job I've ever had in my life.

Inoki brought me over to Japan again for the celebration of 30 years of combat sports: boxing, wrestling, everything. Many have called the match between Inoki and me the best match of all time, or at least in the last 30 years. And it was just after my knee operation; I could hardly get in the ring and stand up.

Yuko Miyato had gotten in touch with me even before Inoki. I was in Las Vegas working as a security guard, and I was coaching other security guards. He sent for me to go to Japan. I did an exhibition match with Nick Bockwinkel. I was in no shape to do it, and neither was Nick, but we went over and did it on one of the big UWFi fight cards.

After that, Miyato asked me to go to Nashville and coach the UWFi guys from America and other places who were sent there. They'd fly me over to Japan four or five times a year just to be at the matches. The fighters would come to Tennessee to work out with me. Guys like Billy Scott, Gary Albright, and Gene Lydick used to come and work out. Then that split up because, in Japan, when guys get good enough, they split up and form their own promotions. At that time, in the early '90s, I think there were probably close to 39 or 40 different promotion companies in Japan that were coaching real catch wrestling and submission fighting. Every wrestler that had been taught by Karl

Gotch or by me was a champion—Miyato, Takada, and others.

Through Miyato, I became the head coach of the UWFi, and that's where I got to teach Sakuraba, Takada, Tamura, Inoue, and many more of those guys. The UWFi brought in Lou Thesz because he had the belt and was a famous name, but I coached them. Then I became the head coach of the Snake Pit Gym and lived in Japan for 15 years. Miyato really saved me because I had started to drink too much and put on too much weight as a result of the divorce. On top of that, my knees and hip all had to be replaced, my nervous system was wrecked from years of wrestling, and I couldn't train anymore.

Visiting a hospital in Japan at Christmas.

It was because of people like Miyato that other people realized that I was still around. For example, when I was in Japan, Jake Shannon asked me to come back to the United States to do a seminar on catch wrestling; that was because of Miyato. I've got to thank Miyato very much, as well as all the other Japanese people that helped me over there.

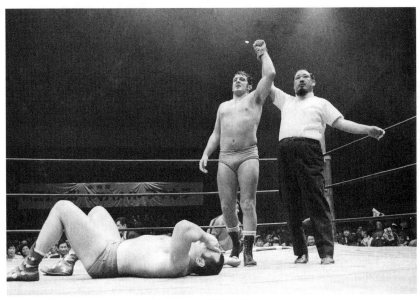

Another victory in Japan, this time of Sean Reagan.

Coaching the Japanese wasn't easy because they had a mindset that we've never had in catch wrestling. They were used to the belt system, where a brown belt goes up against a black belt, and if there are outsiders watching, that brown belt will not do anything against the black belt. The brown belt has to lose because of their custom. Well, in wrestling, we don't have that. I mean, if you can beat the best guy when you're on the mat, you beat him. So the mindset is a lot different.

The way that things are taught is also different. When people come to my trainings, we teach concepts. We're not teaching how you do a technique. In the Japanese cultural system, teaching is a 1-2-3-4-5 process. If you're going

Billy Robinson and Karl Gotch sightseeing in Japan.

to nail two pieces of wood together, one, you put the pieces of wood where you want them. Two, you pick up the nail. Three, you put the nail on the wood. Four, you pick up the hammer. Five, you hit the nail. There was no way a Japanese guy would pick the hammer up first; he'd do it as he's taught. That's how they teach jiujitsu and judo in all the schools that they have. People here are beginning to learn in the Japanese style, too.

But in real fighting, and in a real contest of catch wrestling, there's no one way to do a thing. That's why catch wrestlers were the best. It's because everybody reacts differently. I may go for a single leg on you, on Karl Gotch, or on Billy Joyce, and when I go for it, I'll do it the same way, but each of their reactions will be different. If I've been taught the 1-2-3-4 style, I'll follow the set pattern that I've been taught and fail, whereas in catch wrestling we're above that. We'll say, "Oh, that's a lot of work, now. I'll do this." I may change the angle or I may change to something else, which is why it's called catch-as-catch-can.

THE MMA

Mixed Martial Arts really got started with Antonio Inoki fighting Muhammad Ali. Inoki was trained by Gotch, and I've wrestled and worked out with him. To me, Inoki was the best of all the Japanese guys of that time. After fighting Muhammad Ali, Inoki wrestled Aslam in Pakistan, followed by different boxers and different martial artists. That's really where MMA started, and then promoters got interested in it.

I thank God for the Gracies, because when they took over there were no catch-as-catch-can wrestlers left. That's when everybody was calling the old catch wrestling moves a "Gracie triangle," a "Gracie Kimura," etc. That pissed off a lot of the old-time wrestlers. They came down to the different amateur championships and picked up guys, showed them submissions for MMA, and then the grapplers started taking over everything. Basically, it was because all of the real catch wrestlers (not the show wrestlers) had retired or were injured that the Gracie style of jiu-jitsu was really allowed to peak.

Unfortunately, what is happening now is that guys pick up a few finishing holds—like a double wristlock or a few neck cranks—and they call themselves catch wrestlers. It's like they only know the first chapter of a thousand-chapter book. There are so many different ways to beat a guy. There are so many submissions on the arms and the neck, the legs, the hips, the stretches, the splits and all kinds of front-face locks, cross-faces, if you know how to do them right. Nobody is doing that now, because none of the old-timers are around to show them how to do it.

When amateur wrestlers and folkstyle wrestlers get cross-faced, or grovited, for the first time in our seminars, the usual response is "Shit, I didn't know that was the way you did that." An amateur wrestling champion said he knew how to ride a guy, but he'd learned the amateur style. Then, when I showed him how to get the legs in and how to keep them in, he said it was so easy. He didn't realize it was that easy to get a man and to control him, and that's just one little thing. Catch wrestling is physical chess. With two tough guys, it's like a chess game.

There are a lot of Japanese names that were very tough guys—Maeda, Fujiwara, Fujinami, and others.

Fujiwara was another of Karl's boys who came along after Inoki and who might have been even better than Inoki, but I don't know, because I never saw them actually wrestle each other. Fujiwara was younger than Inoki, and was coming up after I'd left Japan. Fujinami, too, could look after himself very well.

Billy in a match with Sugiyama.

Sakuraba and Tamura were two of my boys. Tamura had a big head, he had an attitude, and he thought he was God's gift to MMA. The problem with him was that he didn't learn the basics well. Tamura was more experienced than Sakuraba when they first started. When they had their early matches, Tamura could beat Sakuraba. But then Sakuraba came into his own and beat everybody.

Sakuraba had learned his basics very well with Shozo Sasahara as his coach in his high school days. To me, Sasahara is one of the greatest amateur wrestlers of all time, technique-wise; he was an Olympic gold medallist and world champion and a very good friend of mine. As a matter of fact, out of all the great amateur wrestlers that I've either seen or wrestled against and beaten, Sasahara is the closest to a Wigan-style wrestler. The only difference was that he didn't know the submissions.

When I started training Sakuraba, he was Takada's underling. So anytime Takada was there, which was every day, Sakuraba would do all his sparring and everything with Takada. While anybody was there, Takada would beat the living shit out of Sakuraba. It's a Japanese custom, like I said earlier. I complained about it a little bit and took Sakuraba to the side (on *a lot of different occasions*) and told him to try different things. Well, things started to work for him with other guys, but he still wouldn't really try anything with Takada, out of custom.

Such bullying happens not just in Japan, but everywhere when people become the boss and the promoter. Take Verne Gagne, for example. He was the AWA world champion, but he always had guys, like Karl Gotch and me, who were policemen for him. Before he brought me in, it was Baron von Raschke. After I left AWA, it was Khosrow Vaziri, then Brad Rheingans, whom I had trained and who was also a great amateur wrestler. Gagne always had a person around him who took care of matters. He didn't have the submission experience, or the stamina, because he didn't believe in sparring a lot. His idea was to get everybody tired, and then he'd come on the mat with them at the end and beat the shit out of them when they were dead beat.

Billy in victory over Karl Gotch.

Well, Karl couldn't stand that, and when I did the camps, I wouldn't stand for that, either. I did everything that I asked all the students to do, which was the style at Wigan and was Gotch's style, too. You just don't take advantage of somebody. You don't make them bridge when they've never bridged before. It'll ruin their necks. There are bullies all around the world. That sort of stuff doesn't happen just in Japan.

Anyway, I think that the groupings—UWF, the UWFi, Pancrase, etc.—were great. The only real problem that I ever really had with them was very simple. When they formed these organizations, they should have had pinfalls. Lou Thesz and Danny Hodge thought so, too. Now, that was the biggest mistake they've ever made, because it is far more entertaining for the audience to watch a guy fighting off his back who doesn't want to get into the guard position because he might lose by being pinned.

When a guy is fighting off his back to try and escape, that's when you get a lot more different opportunities to get arm submissions, neck submissions, and ankle submissions and get into riding positions.

Billy and his tag team partner Wahoo McDaniels.

They've really cut out 50 percent of the sport by not having pinfalls. I think that MMA will finally turn around and realize that you need pinfalls to make it more exciting. Then, when people are fighting out of pinfalls, they will leave themselves open for striking, kicking, kneeing, and submissions—my style.

Mixed Martial Arts fighters are now being educated to know chokes, submissions, and knockouts, and that's a start. A great boxer doesn't go out to try and force a knockout. He'll go out and fight; the knockout will come to him. A catch-as-catch-can wrestler is the same. I don't go chasing a submission—which is exactly what it seems everybody who calls themselves a "catch wrestler" is doing now. I go out and wrestle catch until the submission comes my way. Like, for instance, take the collar and elbow—that's where you grab the guy behind his neck. He grabs you and you hook your arm over the elbow, and you're pulling and pushing. It used to be one of the more basic things in the old style of amateur wrestling, but not so much now, because they bend over a lot and go to defend the legs. Well, one thing you can do is when he grabs you behind the head, you grab the fingers and pull them off. The guy will grab you again. This time you don't block it. You allow him to grab you. Then, a little bit later, you take his hand off. You allow him to grab you again. After a little while, you can see he's not worried about grabbing you, because he feels safe. That's the time you say thank you, take his hand off as he comes to grab you, knock his arm up, take a single leg, change to a double leg, and pick him up and drive him through the mat as hard as you can. Then you can end it with whatever submission is available. I've set him up in such a way that I can do all that from his just grabbing my neck.

If that doesn't happen, I'm not worried, because I've got so many more things that I can do, and I'm trying to set him up. It's like I want to set up a guy to put his leg out. Every time I take him down, I drive into him on the opposite side so that he'll stick his leg out to push back into me to stop me from rolling him over. I'll do that many times, and then, when the time is right, I'll make as if I want to do the same thing. He's going to stick his leg out again, but instead of pushing against him, this time I dive over the top and cradle him. These are very basic examples of how catch wrestling is truly physical chess.

Mixed Martial Arts has improved a lot in the last 10 years because they're starting to learn how to learn. Ten years ago, I was telling everybody about the importance of knowing how to stand up. Right now, people are standing back, looking at a guy to see if he's fallen down or not. You can't do that in a fight. Nowadays, at least some of the top strikers are learning more about the real boxing standard and moving away from the Muay Thai square-shoulder stance, which really just makes for a big, open target. But we're talking about things that MMA's improving on only now; catch wrestlers were masters at these things in the '20s and '30s and for a hundred years before.

Distance, too, is becoming better. The idea is that I want to get close enough for you to either grab me or for me to grab you and do what I want to you. A guy like Billy Joyce would put himself in position so that you would grab him or go for him, and he'd beat you from it. That's catch-as-catch-can. I was brought up with my dad and uncle, with street fighting, with good pro boxing and great catch-as-catch-can wrestling. It's all been mostly forgotten, but now it's coming back, and they're picking up things from old-timers that are telling them, "Try this and try that." There're so many techniques from catch wresting that can improve any MMA fighter if he just learns the basics and doesn't limit himself to a few submissions.

CHAPTER SIX

PHYSICAL CHESS

In my seminars and camps, I get coaches from different gyms or different styles, like jiu-jitsu. Sometimes what they say makes me cringe. They say things like, "If he did this to me, I'd do that." Or, "He can't do this to me, because if he tried, I would do that." What a load of nonsense! Top grapplers, and top catch wrestlers especially, don't plan what they're going to do. They don't know when they're going to do what. I mean if I knew what a guy was going to do, I could stop anybody from doing anything. So why train? Why practise? In catch wrestling, the reason why we can beat any of the other martial arts sports is that we can adjust better. If I go to do something, as soon as I see you are trying to do your counter, I'll be countering that. I'll always be two or three steps ahead of you. Not only that, each fighter reacts differently—I may react to a move in one way, Gordienko may react in another way—so you cannot have a set plan. That's what is difficult to explain to people these days. One Wigan old-timer said to me, "Billy, you never know what's going to happen. If you want to trick somebody, one rule of thumb is put the obvious forward and do the opposite."

Billy Riley puts it in another way: "You break your opponent, take him down, get control. Put him in a position where there are four ways to get out of it. You close three of those doors. There's only one way for him to come out. You just keep those three doors closed until he attempts to come out this way. Sooner

Billy and George Gordienko after having wrestled to a draw in Japan.

or later he'll figure that that's the way out, and when he tries to come out that way, you say thank you and beat him."

In the old days, it was fun to go down to the gym and listen to the stories of four different generations and their champions. They'd describe funny things that happened in different matches. It was just great. I would love catch-as-catch-can wrestling to become an Olympic sport and a professional sport—a legitimate, professional sport with pinfalls and submissions, and reasonable time allowances, maybe one-hour time limits. You can have shorter time limits in the preliminary matches.

Now, with matches cut down to three two-minute rounds or so, everything has become about power. You can train a 240-pound guy to be exceptionally powerful for two minutes, but it doesn't make him a good wrestler. If you get him on the mat and wrestle for 15 or 20 minutes, all his power will be gone. His extra power from the extra weight will be gone.

These days, almost everybody's coming into combat sports through the Japanese style of learning, with the belt system. That's what is great about Jake's and my idea about the certification. It wouldn't have been necessary in the old days, but it's necessary now. It helps create an interest among all those people who want to come to a seminar and get a certificate, so we can actually teach them the old catch-as-catch-can way—to learn how to learn. And I can't blame them for wanting to have their names noted as part of the history of catch-as-catch-can.

There are a lot of old-timers who I haven't mentioned here that people have just forgotten about. Martial artists from the '20s and '30s were better at catch wrestling and boxing than the guys now, simply because there was a lot more of them. But there was no publicity, even in the late 1800s. I've asked guys at the certification camps about George Hackenschmidt, and some have never heard of him. Hackenschmidt was a huge name in catch-as-catch-can, like a Jack Dempsey or a Rocky Marciano was in boxing. All those guys learned their greatness from people who came before them, and those people learned from people who came before them. But none of the names were recorded back in those days.

Catch-as-catch-can wrestling is no doubt the greatest sport in the world. You learn humility. You learn discipline. You learn to respect others. You are humbled when you begin learning the sport. You realize that everybody who gets on the mat and practises this sport does it because they love it; it's tough, it's hard on the body, and if they still come down to the gym to be your sparring partner, it's because they love it. You have respect for that. You don't say somebody is a piece of shit. You will not allow anybody to talk bad or do anything bad to those people who actually get on the mat. Catch-as-catch-can is a knowledge sport. It's a fun sport. That's why I call it physical chess. It was so much fun, and nobody complained about injuries. They'd just tape it up because they just wanted to get on the mat. It was like a great brotherhood. There was no brotherhood like it.

Now, it's like people have lost the discipline, knowledge, and humility of knowing that on any given day, anybody can be the best. That's what you learn in catch-as-catch-can wrestling. It's like life. It's not all ups and it's not all downs. If you are a multi-millionaire, you cannot say, "I'll be a multi-millionaire for life"; the market may fall, and you get members of big, powerful families committing suicide or whatever. Catch-as-catch-can wrestling is like that. Even when you are the best, you know it's not going to last forever.

THANK YOU

BILLY ROBINSON

I would like to say thanks to the people that really helped me at the end of my pro career—Miyato and the Snake Pit Gym in Koenji, Tokyo, Japan, and sport reporters Koji and Fumi Sato, who helped me a lot and who I am still in touch with. Jake Shannon, you and Sondra and the kids are like my own family. I'd like to thank Josh Barnett and Erik Paulson and to wish Josh success as a competitor—he's great. Thanks to Harry Smith (one of my new boys) and Billy Scott, too. Thank you to Drew Price, Matt Hamilton, and Roli Delgado, who welcomed me with open arms in Arkansas. Last, but not least, thanks to my son, Spencer, and his wife,

Mary Alyce, who put up with me and looked after me during the surgeries on both knees and one hip—that had to be tough.

JAKE SHANNON

Very special thanks to Billy Robinson for so selflessly sharing with me his knowledge of the history and techniques of catch-as-catch-can wrestling over the years. Also, thank you to C. Nathan Hatton and Liza Joseph for their critical review of my work. I would also like to thank every single patron of ScientificWrestling. com for supporting our efforts to document and share the ideas of catch-as-catch-can. I would also like to thank my wife, Sondra, with whom I've been able to pursue my dreams.

At ECW Press, we want you to enjoy this book in whatever format you like, whenever you like. Leave your print book at home and take the eBook to go! Purchase the print edition and receive the eBook free. Just send an email to ebook@ecwpress.com and include:

- the book title
- the name of the store where you purchased it
- your receipt number
- your preference of file type: PDF or ePub?

A real person will respond to your email with your eBook attached. And thanks for supporting an independently owned Canadian publisher with your purchase!

Get the eBook free!